# Making sense of Christian art & architecture

# Making sense of Christian art & architecture

**Heather Thornton McRae**

 Thames & Hudson

First published in the United Kingdom in 2015 by

Thames & Hudson Ltd,
181A High Holborn,
London WC1V 7QX

This book was designed and produced by
Quintessence Editions Ltd.
The Old Brewery,
6 Blundell Street,
London, N7 9BH

| | |
|---|---|
| Project Editor | Juliet Lough |
| Editor | Fiona Plowman |
| Designer | Josse Pickard |
| Production Manager | Anna Pauletti |
| Editorial Director | Jane Laing |
| Publisher | Mark Fletcher |

British Library Cataloguing-in-Publication Data
A catalogue record for this book is available from
the British Library

ISBN 978-0-500-29170-2

Printed in China

To find out about all our publications, please visit
**www.thamesandhudson.com**.

There you can subscribe to our e-newsletter, browse or download
our current catalogue, and buy any titles that are in print.

# Contents

# Introduction

Two thousand years of Christianity have inspired some of the most important works of art and architecture known to humankind. They span not just time, but also the world.

Almost all religious traditions need a place to worship, but Christianity also requires a space for contemplation. This defining aspect of the religion created a vibrant monastery tradition. Monasteries include churches, but their underlying principle is different because they provide for every aspect of life, allowing monks to be apart from the world. They also demonstrate Christianity's preference for a communal form of monasticism.

Christian spaces of worship and contemplation were often embellished with multiple art forms. In the earliest centuries these tended to be part of the buildings themselves. Painted frescoes, stone and glass mosaics, stone and wood carvings and even stained glass decorated many walls, floors, and ceilings. In the 6th century, Pope Gregory the Great noted that, in a time of declining literacy, these images served 'to instruct the minds of the ignorant'. Then more portable forms of religious art appeared, including paintings and free-standing sculpture. Devotional objects – the chalice and pyx holding the wine and bread of the Eucharist, the censer used to burn incense at Mass, rosary beads, reliquaries protecting remains of the saints – were made into works of art, often by the foremost artists and artisans of their day.

One of the most important physical expressions of Christianity is the codex, or book. The first Christian texts were probably written on papyrus, the medium of antiquity. When papyrus supplies became irregular during the decline of the Roman Empire, Christians turned to writing on prepared animal skins, known as parchment. When the 'pages' were bound into books to make them more durable, Christian practices became focused on the books of the Bible. Each book has its own importance and interpretations, but none more so than the four Gospels of the New Testament, because they record the events of Jesus's life and death. Books, rather than being incidental, were seen to be as necessary as churches, monasteries, and liturgical objects. Indeed, many Gospel books and other works were used as liturgical texts in the services. While the words remained important after the advent of the printing press, not having to copy each Bible or religious text by hand changed the nature of the art form.

Informing all of the forms of Christian art and architecture is the theme of death. The role of death is seminal in Christianity because of the central tenet of Christ's death on the cross and his subsequent resurrection and second coming. Death's place in Christianity is further assured by the belief that Christ will return at the end of the world, as told in Matthew 25 and the Book of Revelation, and that, during the Apocalypse, he will sit in judgment of all mankind, deciding who will join him and who will be sent to oblivion. This focus on the eternal soul led to sarcophagi, church monuments, frescoes, sculptures and books with themes relating to different aspects of Christian death, and the death and resurrection of Christ.

Together with the sacraments of communion and baptism and the primacy of the Gospels, the reality of death established the theological and iconographical foundation of Christian art and architecture, but the nuanced differences between Roman Catholic, Eastern Orthodox, Coptic, Protestant and other forms of Christianity gave rise to variations on the underlying theme. Those variations led to works of art emphasizing aspects as different as the role of Mary, the ideal of simplicity, personal devotion to God and even the end of the world. They also shine in even the most simple and humble Christian architectural and artistic forms, reminding us that potentially there are as many variations in Christian art and architecture as there are individual believers.

# Places of Worship

# House Church

c. 240 CE  **Dura-Europos, Syria**

**ABANDONED** 256 CE  **MATERIAL** Mud brick
**ASSEMBLY ROOM** 5×13 m/16×42 ft  **TOTAL AREA** 17×19 m/57×62 ft

The earliest Christian churches were not a distinct architectural form, but instead were the more discreet private homes of wealthy converts. Some of these houses were donated and were outfitted to serve specific religious needs. Dura-Europos, a small Roman military city of about 7,000, was largely destroyed and abandoned in 256 CE after the Persians conquered it. However, in 1920 British troops discovered the town, largely buried under rubble that had preserved portions of the city. Along the west wall archaeologists found three houses that had been converted for religious worship: a Mithraeum, a synagogue and a church. The synagogue and church are the oldest known in the world. The house was built in the traditional Roman plan, with rooms surrounding a central courtyard. Two of the smaller rooms were turned into a large assembly room for worship (with a capacity for 65 people), with a small raised area at the east end. This room was undecorated. The real treasures were found in another room, rebuilt as a baptistery and containing a font large enough for full-body immersion. The walls of the baptistery are decorated with frescoes, including the oldest painted representations of Jesus in the world: the Good Shepherd, the healing of the paralytic and walking on water. Accompanying scenes include several from the New Testament, as well as David and Goliath. Most of the Christian frescoes and artefacts are now held in a museum at Yale University in the United States, but, sadly, the city has recently been looted and destroyed by heavy machinery during the chaos resulting from the Sunni separatist state in Syria and the Syrian Civil War.

### Frescoes

The figural representations of Christ in the baptistery at Dura-Europos belong to the Hellenistic Jewish iconographic tradition. They are probably the earliest Christian paintings. They show that early Christians had already tacitly decided that depictions of Christ were acceptable and did not violate the prohibition of 'graven images'. This fresco illustrates the story of Christ walking on water.

'The meaning of what appears on walls like those of this baptistery becomes clear only when we remember what happened between them.'
MICHAEL PEPPARD, ACADEMIC

# Church of the Holy Sepulchre

4th century CE **Jerusalem**

**COMMISSIONED BY** Constantine I **CONSECRATED** c. 325 CE
**AFFILIATION** Various Christian churches **MATERIALS** Stone, wood

Located in the Christian Quarter of Old Jerusalem, the Church of the Holy Sepulchre occupies the holiest site in Christianity. Under its roof are both the Aedicule, the tomb in which Christ is traditionally believed to have been buried and risen from the dead, and Golgotha (Calvary), the site of his crucifixion. Emperor Hadrian built a temple to Venus on the site in the 2nd century, but Constantine ordered it replaced in 325 by a church. The first church was damaged and repaired a number of times before being destroyed in 1009. Byzantine Emperor Constantine IX Monomachos financed a new building that was completed in 1048. This new building stood when the Crusaders took Jerusalem in 1099, and they began renovations that were finished by Queen Melisende in 1149, before Saladin retook the city in 1187. Control of the church under the Ottomans vacillated between the Franciscans and the Orthodox from 1555 until 1767, when it was decreed by firman that they share the building, a compromise still in existence today. Modern renovations have been ongoing since 1959. One of the most impressive architectural features is the large dome that allows light to enter over the rotunda housing the tomb. Formed by carefully removing the rock around the tomb, the Aedicule is now composed of two rooms: the tomb itself and a room with the rock the angel rolled away at the Resurrection. Franciscans and Orthodox clerics take turns holding services, while each has chapels and altars of its own within the building.

### Christ Pantocrator

A second, smaller dome was constructed over the Katholicon, which is the space reserved for the Greek Orthodox Church. It is adorned with Byzantine-style mosaics depicting Christ Pantocrator (Christ Almighty).

'At the place where Jesus was crucified, there was a garden, and in the garden a new tomb, in which no one had ever been laid. Because it was the Jewish day of Preparation and since the tomb was nearby, they laid Jesus there.'

JOHN 19:41–42

# Hagia Sophia

537 CE **Istanbul, Turkey**

**ARCHITECTS** Isidore of Miletus, Anthemius of Tralles   **MATERIALS** Porphyry stone, marble, rock, mosaics   **DIMENSIONS** 82 x 73 x 55 m/270 x 240 x 180 ft

The Nika riots in Constantinople (modern-day Istanbul) in 532 CE left thousands dead and the city in ruins. After quelling the riots, Roman Emperor Justinian I built the Hagia Sophia, or Church of Holy Wisdom, to replace the destroyed imperial cathedral. The new basilica was built on the square plan distinctive of Byzantine architecture. Massive in scale, it was topped by a dome so heavy that the walls collapsed. When reinforced and rebuilt, the building was so large that it was only surpassed in size by the Pantheon in Rome. Designed to be the seat of the Orthodox patriarch of Constantinople, Justinian's church had specially designed balconies that provided perfect acoustics for choirs. Magnificent mosaics originally covered the walls, but these were plastered over when the Ottomans converted the basilica to a mosque in 1453, later adding four minarets. The Hagia Sophia is renowned for its remarkable 'floating dome', which took five years and ten months to complete. Built of bricks and mortar, the dome was initially perfectly round. Although centuries of subsequent repairs have affected its shape, its visual and spiritual impact remains. The massive dome is said to be floating because of the row of windows at its base which, when the sun is shining, give the illusion that the dome is floating on a cloud of light. Worshippers felt that they were able to glimpse heaven while still on earth, and this feeling was compounded when choirs placed in upper balconies sang, creating the impression that angels were calling to them from above. Since 1931, when Hagia Sophia ceased to be a mosque, the building has been a museum.

## Pantheon Dome

The dome of Rome's Pantheon – its oculus (circular hole) open to the sky – rivals that of the Hagia Sophia in terms of influence. The height to the oculus and the dome's diameter are the same: 43 m (142 ft). Completed in 126, it remains the world's largest unreinforced concrete dome.

'The dome is a work admirable and terrifying... seeming not to rest on the masonry below it, but to be suspended by a chain of gold from the height of the sky.'
PROCOPIUS OF CAESAREA, BYZANTINE SCHOLAR

# Church of San Juan Bautista

7th century CE **Baños de Cerrato, Castile and León, Spain**

**COMMISSIONED BY** King Recceswinth **CONSECRATED** 661 CE
**DIMENSIONS** 20 x 13 m/66 x 43 ft **MATERIALS** Ashlar stone blocks

### Recceswinth's Votive Crown

King Recceswinth also commissioned a gold votive crown, a form of religious offering, that could be hung by chains and displayed. A part of the buried Treasure of Guarrazar, it was discovered near Toledo, the Visigoth capital, in 1859.

'RECCESVINTVVS REX OFFERET [King Recceswinth offered this].'

LETTERS ON RECCESWINTH'S VOTIVE CROWN

When the Visigothic King of Spain Recceswinth was injured after battling Basque forces, he went to the Roman hot baths in the central Spanish province of Palencia where his injuries were healed. In thanks, in 661 CE Recceswinth ordered a monastery built in the name of St John the Baptist. While the rest of the monastery no longer exists, the church still stands in the town of Baños de Cerrato as the oldest surviving example of a Visigoth church. Made of ashlar stone blocks and without mortar (drywall), the Church of San Juan Bautista is one of the last western European examples of ashlar masonry until the age of Charlemagne and marks the end of Roman building practices as late antiquity gave way to the Middle Ages. Although the building is small, its architecture incorporates a number of important architectural details. It has barrel vaulting and eight marble Corinthian columns, four on each side, separating the two side aisles from the central nave. At the front, it has an apse with a small room to each side: the diaconium and the prothesis. The diaconium was used to robe the deacons while the prothesis was used by virgins to prepare the unleavened bread used in services. These two rooms are required for the original liturgy used by the Visigoths, who were a nomadic tribe of the Germanic Goths. This type of service remained in Spain after the Muslim conquest in 711 as the Mozarab Liturgy until the Reconquest of Spain allowed Roman Catholics to update the liturgy in the 12th century.

# Cathedral of Córdoba

*c.* 1520–1600 CE **Cordóba, Spain**

**COMMISSIONED BY** Bishop Alonso Manrique **ARCHITECTS** Hernán Ruiz I, Hernán Ruiz II, Juan de Ochoa **MATERIALS** Granite, wood, marble

The Cathedral of Córdoba, which was recognized as a UNESCO World Heritage Site in 1984, is built on a site that has been sacred for more than 2,000 years. Replacing a Roman temple to the god Janus, the Visigoths built a church in around 550. After the conquest by Muslim forces in 711, the space was divided in two, between Christian and Muslim worshippers. When the Muslim population needed a bigger space, Muslim leaders allowed the Christians to build a new church elsewhere and constructed the famous Mosque of Córdoba. The building's final major change was to become a Catholic cathedral in 1239, after King Fernando III captured Córdoba in 1236. Much of the mosque, however, remained intact. Initially, almost no architectural changes were made; instead, various parts of the mosque were used as chapels, altars were installed, and the minaret was used as a bell tower. The biggest architectural alteration occurred in the 16th century, when a large Renaissance church, with Mannerist details such as an oval dome, was built in the centre of the mosque. The *maqsura* (where the caliph prayed) and the *mihrab* (noting the direction of Mecca) were left untouched, but part of the centre was lost. However, this destruction of a small fraction of the mosque is probably what saved it from complete destruction by the Spanish Inquisition. Additions to the structure continued until the late 18th century, including the installation in 1747 of elaborate mahogany choir stalls constructed by the Baroque artist Pedro Duque y Cornejo, located around the high altar. The stalls depict biblical scenes from the Old Testament and the Gospels.

### Aerial shot

This aerial photo shows where the arcaded hypostyle hall of the mosque is interrupted by the buttresses and soaring nave and dome of the cathedral that rise above it. From above, the viewer has a sense of the vast scale of the mosque, which sprawls over a surface area of 23,000 square metres (248,000 sq ft). At its apogee, it was the second largest mosque in the Islamic world. The design is similar to that of the Great Mosque of Damascus.

'You have taken something unique in all the world and destroyed it to build something you can find in any city.'

KING CHARLES V OF CASTILE AND ARAGON

# St Basil's Cathedral

1555–61 CE **Moscow, Russia**

**COMMISSIONED BY** Ivan the Terrible   **AFFILIATION** Russian Orthodox
**MATERIALS** Brick, stucco   **HEIGHT** 60 m/197 ft

## Chapel Interior

Westerners are frequently surprised by the interior of St Basil's. With its subdivision into nine original chapels, it is a warren of narrow stairways, arches, intricate decoration and icons, completely unlike the open basilica plans most commonly found in the West.

'This cathedral is a shrine and a symbol of Russia.'

ANDREY BUSYGIN, RUSSIAN DEPUTY CULTURE MINISTER

St Basil's Cathedral was commissioned by Ivan the Terrible to celebrate his capture of the Tatar capital Kazan in 1552 on the feast of the Intercession of the Mother of God, making its official name the Cathedral of the Protection of Most Holy Theotokos on the Moat. When St Basil (Vasily) was buried at the church in 1588, it gained the name by which it is better known. St Basil's actually consists of nine churches, with eight smaller ones grouped around the largest, the Church of the Intercession. A tenth church was added to house St Basil's tomb. Inside, visitors are met by a labyrinthine subdivision of space, including narrow vaulted corridors and a series of small passages and rooms. The influences on the exterior architecture are a subject of great debate, but they are most likely a reflection of traditional Russian wood churches, Italian brick vaulting and the Kazan Qolsharif Mosque, the symbol of Kazan that was destroyed in 1552. Originally, the cathedral was white with gilded onion domes, but about 200 years ago, bright colours were added. St Basil's has narrowly missed destruction on a number of occasions, most famously when Napoleon Bonaparte tried and failed to set explosive charges to destroy it in 1812. With the advent of communism, Soviet leaders debated demolishing the complex in order to create a large military parade ground on Red Square, but eventually compromised by converting it into a museum. In bad shape at the collapse of the Soviet Union in 1991, St Basil's has seen some restoration in recent years. It is now the State Historical Museum, but occasional services are now conducted there by the Russian Orthodox Patriarch.

## Tracery

A key Gothic element of St Luke's is the tracery on some of the windows. While the church's builders utilized the more readily available brick, the original tracery used to divide window panes in Europe was stone and the windows were stained glass.

'That whosoever shall absent himselfe from divine service any Sunday without an allowable excuse shall forfeit a pound of tobacco, and he that absenteth himselfe a month shall forfeit 50lb. of tobacco.'

GENERAL ASSEMBLY OF VIRGINIA, MARCH 1623

# St Luke's Church

17th century **Smithfield, Virginia, USA**

**AFFILIATION** Protestant   **MATERIALS** Brick, stained glass
**DIMENSIONS** 9 x 20 m/29 x 66 ft   **THICKNESS OF WALLS** 1m/3 ft

When English colonists began settling in Virginia, they brought with them a need for a house of worship. St Luke's Church, also known as the Old Brick Church, was constructed in the 17th century to fulfil this need. The traditional date cited is 1632, which would make it the oldest church of English construction in the United States. However, it is more likely that it was built between the 1660s and 1680s. This dating would still make it the oldest existing church of English construction. While the exact date is uncertain, the influence of Colonel Joseph Bridger on the church's construction is clear. Coming from England in the 1650s, he brought with him Jacobean taste that can be seen in the interior Tuscan columns formed from the trunk of a tree and the turned balusters of the rood screen and kneeling rail. The church's exterior is considered to be at the end of the English Gothic tradition, but made of brick instead of stone. This Gothic style is seen in the exterior buttresses, stepped gables, brick 'tracery' windows and the interior tie-beam timber roof construction. The Old Brick Church experienced hard times during the American Revolution, with British troops setting up temporary camp in the grounds in 1781, and even more difficult ones when the church was turned into the stables for Confederate forces during the American Civil War in 1861. It was officially named St Luke's Episcopal Church in 1820, but was abandoned in 1832 in favour of a new parish church. By 1960, St Luke's had been designated a US National Historic Landmark and today it is used once more for Episcopal weddings and services.

# San Miguel Mission

1610–26 CE **Santa Fe, New Mexico, USA**

**STYLE** Spanish colonial **AFFILIATION** Roman Catholic
**MATERIALS** Adobe, wood **DIMENSIONS** 24 x 10 x 8 m / 79 x 33 x 26 ft

The San Miguel Mission, also known as the San Miguel Chapel, is considered to be the oldest church in continual use in the United States. The Spanish colonial mission church was built soon after Santa Fe became the administrative capital of what is present-day New Mexico. The Franciscan missionary Fray Alonso de Benavides was appointed *custos*, or head of the Order, and travelled from Mexico to Santa Fe to take up his post. With him were 1,000 men, most of whom were Mexican natives, probably Tlaxcalan, who built the church. A church in the capital was necessary not only for the Spaniards and Mexicans with him, but also for the local peoples, such as the Pueblo, because King Philip had declared in 1573 that colonists were to maintain good relations with the indigenous peoples. San Miguel was only one of roughly fifty mission churches built in native areas by Spain in the 17th century. The original building was badly damaged during the Pueblo Revolt of 1680 and rebuilt in 1710 following the Spanish Reconquest. The original adobe walls are a massive 1.5 metres (5 ft) thick and they were heavily buttressed during rebuilding. Built in a typical Spanish colonial style, San Miguel Mission includes a flat roof and vigas – logs that have been stripped of bark but unhewn – which were used as roof beams between the adobe walls. The vigas are still visible on the ceiling from the inside, but only two are original to the 1710 reconstruction. The wooden reredos (altar screen) includes a statue of St Michael dating to around 1709. The building became a US National Historic Landmark in 1968 and is still used for conducting Catholic masses.

## San Francisco de Asís

Another adobe New Mexico church that features vigas in the interior ceiling is the Mission San Francisco de Asís, built between 1772 and 1816, in Ranchos de Taos. Its vigas are supported by wooden corbels and its main altar displays reredos altar screens.

'As soon as I came, I commenced to build the church and monastery – and to the honour and glory of God our Lord, it would shine in whatsoever place.'

FRAY ALONSO DE BENAVIDES, *MEMORIAL* (1630)

## Miagao Church

The Roman Catholic parish church in Miagao, Iloilo Province, Philippines, is another example of the Earthquake Baroque style. Its main facade is renowned for its ornate stone relief sculpture of St Christopher and Christ, a scene that features coconut, papaya and guava shrubs, together with other local details.

'The most enduring impressions are the poignant memories of a tumultuous yet glorious past of a nation, embedded among the layers and heaps of huge stones and bricks that make a church.'

UNESCO

# Paoay Church

1710 CE  **Paoay, Ilocos Norte, Philippines**

**COMMISSIONED BY** Father Antonio Estavillo    **AFFILIATION** Roman Catholic
**MATERIALS** Coral stone, brick, stucco    **DIMENSIONS** 110 x 40 m/361 x 131 ft

Soon after Spanish colonization of the Philippines started in the 16th century, Augustinian friars were the first to evangelize in the islands. When an earthquake destroyed their church at Paoay, Father Antonio Estavillo began rebuilding it in 1694. It was rebuilt in the Earthquake Baroque style of the 17th and 18th centuries — a mixture of what the Spanish priests remembered of the churches of their homeland, combined with native influences and measures to prevent destruction by earthquakes. For stability, Paoay is lower and wider than most European churches of the period, with brick used on the upper structure because it was lighter than the coral stone used on the lower walls. The church also has enormous buttresses at the back and sides of the building for stability, wider and stouter than most European examples. The stair-like buttresses on each side also serve as very steep staircases, perhaps intended for access to the roof. More significantly, the three-storey bell tower, which is made from coral stone, is squat and separate from the main structure of the church in order to prevent damage during earthquakes. The Filipino and Chinese craftsmen who worked on the construction contributed to the building's distinctive flair. These influences can be seen in the curves of the buttresses, the pagoda-like design of the bell tower and the front facade with its curves that are reminiscent of a Javanese stupa. Officially known as the Church of St Augustine, the Paoay Church was declared a National Cultural Treasure by the Philippine government in 1973 and a UNESCO World Heritage Site in 1993. It is still in use today as a Catholic parish church.

# Daqin Pagoda

7th century CE  **Chang'an, Shaanxi, China**

**FOUNDED BY** Tang Dynasty    **MATERIALS** Brick, wood panelling
**HEIGHT** 32 m/105 ft

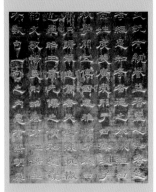

## The Xi'an Stele

The Xi'an Stele was erected in 781 with an inscription composed by the monk Jingjing titled 'The Stele on the Propagation of the Luminous Religion of Daqin in China.' It uses Syriac and holds the name of seventy clergy.

'In the 8th century, when the Da Qin monastery was at its height, the reach of the Eastern Church stretched three times as far as the Church of the West.'

MARTIN PALMER, ALLIANCE OF RELIGIONS AND CONSERVATION

Chang'an, the capital of Tang Dynasty China, began to receive Christian Nestorian missionaries from Persia in the early 7th century. The famous Xi'an Stele, named in honour of Chang'an's modern name, was rediscovered in the early 17th century. It describes the arrival of a monk named Aluoben in 635 who introduced the emperor to Christianity and within three years had obtained permission for it to be spread throughout China. The Daqin Pagoda is believed to be the embodiment of that missionary success. 'Daqin' is a term that can mean 'in the West' and is associated with Christianity in China. The pagoda was the church for a monastery that is no longer in existence, built within the complex of the imperial temple. The seven-storey octagonal pagoda was built in a Chinese style. However, some of the objects inside point to eastern Christian iconography, including a nativity scene executed in mud and plaster with a statue of Mary. There is also graffiti in Syriac, the language of the Eastern Christian Church, on the fourth floor. The non-Western nature of the iconography and the architectural style have led some historians to question its original function, although they are in the minority. After an imperial edict banned all foreign religions in 845, the pagoda was used as a Daoist and then Buddhist temple. It was abandoned in 1556 after it was seriously damaged in an earthquake and many of its underground chambers were sealed. It is the oldest surviving church in China and was placed on the World Monuments Fund watch list after its Christian origins were rediscovered at the end of the 20th century.

# Charlemagne's Palatine Chapel

*c.* 796 CE **Aachen, Germany**

**STYLE** Carolingian Renaissance   **CONSECRATED** 805 CE
**ARCHITECT** Odo of Metz   **DIAMETER** 16.5 m/54 ft   **HEIGHT** 38 m/125 ft

When Charlemagne was crowned Roman Emperor in 800 CE, his coronation had religious significance dating back almost 500 years. Constantine I had called himself the Thirteenth Apostle when he converted to Christianity in the 4th century and he saw a continuing role of religious leadership for the emperor in the new faith. This role continued in Byzantium for more than a millennium, but it was more contested in the West. However, Charlemagne in many ways modelled his imperial role on what he knew of Justinian I from visits to Ravenna and Rome. When he built a palace complex at Aachen at the end of the 8th century, he consciously sought to appropriate the traditional Roman symbols of authority for his Palatine Chapel, the only portion of the palace complex that remains today. Charlemagne wrote to Pope Hadrian requesting marble from Italy and thirty-two decorative columns were shipped from Ravenna and Rome. The octagonal shape of the chapel is drawn from the Basilica of San Vitale in Ravenna, the religious and artistic manifestation of Justinian's religious and earthly powers. The placement of Charlemagne's throne also emphasizes his role. Its original location gave the emperor a direct view of the main altar and the depiction of Christ above it. Architecturally, the addition of a westwork (monumental facade), complete with atrium and towers, became a feature of Western church architecture, although the octagonal shape was one of the last uses of centrally planned churches in the West for centuries.

## Charlemagne's Throne

Charlemagne's marble throne dates to around 800 CE and is still kept in the Palatine Chapel. It was used until 1531 by the Ottonian kings of Germany for their coronations, although Charlemagne himself was not crowned on this throne. Above the main altar, facing the throne, is an image of Christ in Majesty.

'He was a constant worshipper at this church as long as his health permitted, going morning and evening, even after nightfall, besides attending Mass.'

EINHARD, *THE LIFE OF CHARLEMAGNE* (1880)

# Nave of Durham Cathedral

1099–1128 CE **Durham, England, UK**

**COMMISSIONED BY** William of St Carilef   **MATERIALS** Stone, glass
**STYLE** Norman   **DIMENSIONS** 63 x 25 x 22 m (207 x 82 x 72 ft)

### Fan Vaults

An English variation on the Gothic style that partially originated at Durham is fan vaulting, as seen in the Victorian reconstruction of the 1608 ceiling of Bath Abbey. In a fan vault, the ribs of the arch are all of the same curve and are spaced equidistantly to produce a pleasing visual element.

'The architecture of Durham Cathedral is rich in individuality, possessing a character unique among the buildings of its generation.'

STEPHEN GARDNER,
DURHAM UNIVERSITY

The nave, or main body, of Durham Cathedral gives this sacred space a large part of its fame. For centuries previously, churches in the West had been limited by their use of barrel vaulting and groin vaulting; in other words, they had used round, semicircular arches. At Durham, however, the pointed arch was used, together with ribbed vaulting. This is not merely a visual difference, but also allows naves to be built to greater heights, in part because of geometry and in part because the ribs – or visible lines marking where the arches meet in the ceiling – have to be built of strong, thick stone in order to bear the weight of the roof, while the area between the ribs can be built of much lighter material. The ribbed vaulting's height allows the nave to soar three storeys high, including an arcade, a gallery and a clerestory, the latter being the row of windows between the aisle roofline and the ceiling. This innovative use of vaulting and pointed arches marks the transition from the Romanesque architecture of medieval Europe to the Gothic cathedrals that would soon follow. The four enormous piers at the crossing of the nave and the incorporation of a chevron motif are also distinctive features. Originally created to be the seat of the Bishop of Durham and the church for the monastic community there, the cathedral became a Christian Church of the Anglican Communion in 1540 during the Dissolution of the Monasteries. The nave with its groundbreaking stone vaulted ceiling is an architectural milestone and it was designated a UNESCO World Heritage Site in 1986 as part of the Durham World Heritage Site.

## The Monastery of Geghard

The Monastery of Geghard in Armenia is another unique example of a church carved out of living rock. Founded to hold the spear that had allegedly wounded Jesus at the Crucifixion in the 4th century, the monastery continued to expand into the mountain during the 13th century, when the main chapel was built.

'I weary of writing more about these buildings [at Lalibela], because it seems to me that I shall not be believed if I write more.'

FRANCISCO ALVARES, PORTUGUESE MISSIONARY

# Church of St George

12th century CE **Lalibela, Ethiopia**

**COMMISSIONED BY** Lalibela  **AFFLIATION** Ethiopian Orthodox
**MATERIAL** Red volcanic rock  **DIMENSIONS** 25 x 25 x 30 m/82 x 82 x 98 ft

After the fall of Jerusalem to Saladin in 1187, King Gebre Mesqel Lalibela, who ruled in East Africa, ordered the construction of the church of St George. His dynasty, the Zagwe Dynasty, ruled from 900 to 1270 and had previously built a number of monolithic rock-cut churches in the northern Ethiopian town of Roha as it was then known. However, Lalibela's new construction transformed the area, and the town was renamed in his honour. St George, like the other churches in Lalibela, was carved from a single, massive block of living rock, complete with connecting tunnels and an elaborately engineered system to divert rainwater from the buildings and provide water for the inhabitants. King Lalibela intended to turn the town into a 'New Jerusalem', together with renaming the local river the 'Jordan' and designing the other buildings as the heavenly and earthly halves of the city. The heavenly half is in the northern part of the town, and includes the houses of the Saviour, Mary and others. The earthly half is across the river to the south-east and includes the houses of St Mark and Abbot Libanos. St George, the only church hewn in the distinctive cross shape, sits on the heavenly side of the river, to the south-west of the other churches and is considered the finest and best-preserved example. It was probably built by local craftsmen who were influenced by styles that originated from Coptic Egypt and Palestine. Lalibela was chosen as one of the first UNESCO World Heritage Sites of special cultural or physical significance in 1978. However, it is currently in danger due to erosion and the encroachment of the rapidly growing town on the precious site.

# Borgund Stave Church

*c.* 1180 CE **Laerdal, Norway**

**STYLE** Stave church   **AFFILIATION** Church of Norway
**MATERIALS** Vertical wooden boards   **HEIGHT** 37 m/121 ft

When the Borgund Stave Church was built and dedicated to
St Andrew in the second half of the 12th century, Norway's
two-century conversion to Christianity was nearing completion.
The architecture of the stave church combines the native style
with imported Christian features, resulting in a unique form of
Scandinavian Christian architecture. Borgund has typical Christian
church features, such as a nave, apse and chancel, but the
Scandinavian elements are what make it stand out. Built of vertical
wooden boards, or staves, Borgund has six steep-roofed gables for
protection against snow and rain; beautifully carved woodwork
and free-standing wooden posts support the interior of the nave.
Two of the gables are topped with wooden dragon heads, which
are clearly related to carvings on Scandinavian ships. It also has
two runic inscriptions, the longer of which translates as: 'Thorir
carved these runes on the eve of Olaf's Mass, as he travelled past
here. The Norns presented measures of good and evil, great toil
which they created before me.' The norns are the female fates of
Norse mythology, while Thorir dates his inscription according to
the Christian liturgical calendar (St Olaf's Mass). The combination
of pagan and Christian elements shows how permeable the line
of conversion was in Norway and the rest of Scandinavia. While
around 1,000 stave churches were built in Scandinavia before
1350, today only around 30 survive. The earliest stave churches
did not survive because their timbers were inserted into the
ground, causing them to decay, whereas later churches, such as
Borgund, were built upon platforms.

### Oseberg Ship Burial

The dragon-headed gables
at Borgund recall old Norse
traditions, such as this carved
figure from the Oseberg Ship
Burial, discovered in 1904 in
Norway. The grave goods were
placed in the ground *c.* 834,
although they may be even older.

'The stave churches of
Norway are a powerful
and glorious testimony
to a time marked by the
submission of pagan
beliefs to the advent
of Christianity
in Scandinavia.'

MAIA MARIE LANGLEY, AUTHOR

# Sainte-Chapelle

1239–48 CE **Paris, France**

**STYLE** Rayonnant Gothic   **CONSECRATED** 1248   **STYLE** French Gothic
**HEIGHT** 30.5 m/100 ft   **AREA OF STAINED GLASS** 600 sq m/6,458 sq ft

## The Crown of Thorns

According to three of the Gospel accounts, a crown of thorns was placed on the head of Jesus in the events leading up to the Crucifixion. The Crown of Thorns remained at Sainte-Chapelle until the French Revolution, when the relics were dispersed. Eugène Viollet-le-Duc provided it with this neo-Gothic reliquary in the 19th century, when the individual thorns were separated and given their own reliquaries.

'None could doubt but that he owed to these sentiments of purest piety, all those virtues which elevated him, not only above all Kings, but also above all men.'

*THE LIFE OF ST LOUIS*, JEAN DE JOINVILLE (1305–09)

When the Crusades offered Western Christians the opportunity to obtain Byzantine relics, King Louis IX of France obtained one of the most important, the Crown of Thorns, the circlet that was placed on Christ's head during the Passion. It was bought, along with other relics, for 135,000 livres, at a time when Louis' entire income was no more than 250,000 livres a year. In order to have a proper place for these relics, Louis spent another 100,000 livres on an elaborate silver chest to hold them, and 40,000 more to build and glaze Sainte-Chapelle around them, creating in essence the most beautiful reliquary in the world – an entire royal chapel. Built in the Rayonnant Gothic style, the chapel is the oldest surviving portion of the Capetian royal palace on the Ile de la Cité and it houses one of the largest collections of original 13th-century stained glass. However, the chapel was not built out of piety alone. Designed with clear similarities to Charlemagne's Palatine Chapel at Aachen, Sainte-Chapelle was intended to draw favourable comparisons between the two kings. The chapel has a lower level for palace inhabitants, but it was the light-filled upper level, with its deep blue, fleur-de-lis-covered ceiling, that was meant to house the relics. The stained glass is decorated with more than 1,100 biblical figures, as well as a depiction of a barefoot Louis dressed as a penitent and entering Paris with the relics in his hands in 1239. Until Saint-Chapelle was completed in 1248, the relics were stored elsewhere. The chapel was damaged during the French Revolution, after which it served as a filing room until it was restored by architect Eugène Viollet-le-Duc in the 19th century.

# Duomo

1296–1436 CE **Florence, Italy**

**ARCHITECT** Filippo Brunelleschi **MATERIALS** Brick; white, pink and green marble **LENGTH** 153 m/502 ft **HEIGHT** 114 m/376 ft

Officially named the Basilica of Santa Maria del Fiore, the cathedral of Florence is known as 'Il Duomo', derived from the Latin *domus*, meaning 'house of God'. Like most cathedrals, the Duomo took centuries to build: the first stone was laid by Cardinal Valeriana, a papal legate, in 1296 and the structure was completed in 1436. However, the front facade was not completed until the 19th century. The Duomo was begun as a Gothic cathedral to replace the crumbling and too small Cathedral of Saint Reparata. When the original architect, Arnolfo di Cambio died, the work stopped until the Florentine wool merchant's guild, the Arte della Lana, took over patronage in 1331 and appointed Giotto to oversee the construction. After construction was again halted by the Black Death in 1348, the last major wave of construction began in 1418 when the Arte della Lana announced a design competition for building the crowning dome, which was won by Filippo Brunelleschi. He wanted a design that would distinguish Florence from its northern neighbours, such as Milan, and was determined to avoid pointed Gothic arches. Tuscany also did not have enough timber for scaffolding and Brunelleschi's solution was to build a two-shelled dome and use brick, which is much lighter than stone. This enduring symbol of Renaissance Florence was thus created out of necessity and ingenuity. The Duomo is intimately associated with Florentine history, having witnessed Savonarola's preaching and the murder of Giuliano di Piero de' Medici in 1478. Together with the free-standing Baptistery and Giotto's bell tower, the Duomo is a UNESCO World Heritage Site.

## Baptistery Doors

Although artist Lorenzo Ghiberti lost the competition to design the Duomo, he had won the earlier contest in 1401 to design the gilt bronze doors of the Florence Baptistery. The most famous of the low-relief biblical scenes depicted is Abraham sacrificing his son Isaac.

'Only the artist, not the fool, discovers that which nature hides.'

FILIPPO BRUNELLESCHI

# Wawel Cathedral

1364 CE **Kraków, Poland**

**AFFILIATION** Roman Catholic  **MATERIALS** Brick, sandstone, limestone, marble
**BELL TOWER HEIGHT** 40 m/131 ft  **BELL WEIGHT** 9,650 kg/21,274 lb

The first Wawel Cathedral was built on a limestone hill looking over the old town soon after the Bishopric of Kraków was established around 1000 CE, but the current building is the third built on the same spot, after fire damaged the second one in 1305. The current church was built in stages: the chancel foundations soon after the fire; the chancel and ambulatory from 1320 to 1346; and the aisle and body from 1346 to 1364. Even after its consecration, domed side chapels continued to be built for centuries along the exterior walls. The highest point of the cathedral is its bell tower, complete with the Royal Sigismund Bell, which was cast in 1520. While the church still has some of its original Gothic brickwork, it has been reconstructed in a succession of styles, including Italian Renaissance and Baroque. During the age of partitions in the second half of the 18th century, Wawel lost its royal patrons and the cathedral was not well maintained for some time. However, Wawel Cathedral is deeply associated with the kings of Poland: it hosted coronations from the 14th to the 18th century and all but 4 of the 45 kings are buried in the side chapels and crypt. This association soon made it a symbol of Polish nationalism, and from the 19th century, only national heroes have been buried in the 12th-century crypt, including Romantic poet Adam Mickiewicz and Marshal Józef Piłsudski, hero of the period between the world wars. The cathedral is also the location where Karol Wojtyla, the future Pope John Paul II, performed his first Mass in 1946 and was ordained Kraków's auxiliary bishop in 1958.

## St Stanislaus

Associated with Polish national defiance, St Stanislaus was an 11th-century bishop of Kraków, famous for standing up to and being murdered by Bolesław II the Bold. His mausoleum overlooks the centre of the nave and his silver coffin (*c.* 1670) is sculpted with twelve scenes depicting his life and miracles.

'One cannot enter it without a kind of internal trembling, without fear as it encompasses – as few other cathedrals in the world – enormous greatness with which all our history, our past speaks to us.'

KAROL WOJTYLA, FUTURE POPE JOHN PAUL II

# St Peter's Basilica

1506–1626 CE **Vatican City**

**STYLE** Renaissance and Baroque **COMMISSIONED BY** Pope Julius II
**DIMENSIONS** 220 x 150 x 138 m / 722 x 492 x 453 ft **AREA** 2.3 hectares / 5.6 ac.

### St Peter

One of the Apostles and the first bishop, St Peter is regarded as the first pope by Roman Catholics. He is the patron saint of Rome, as well as many occupations, including fishermen and cobblers. His symbol, the keys to the kingdom of heaven, signify the authority he received from Christ.

'You are Peter, and upon this rock I will build my church.... To you I will give the keys of the kingdom of heaven.'

VULGATE BIBLE,
MATTHEW 16:18–19

St Peter's Basilica, the largest church in the world, was designed by some of the foremost figures of the Italian Renaissance, including Donato Bramante, Michelangelo, Carlo Maderno and Gian Lorenzo Bernini. St Peter's replaced a 4th-century church of the same name, both of which reference the tomb of St Peter that is directly below the altar. This association of St Peter and Rome resulted in the city becoming the centre of the Western Catholic Church and its popes. Pope Julius II, desiring a grander tomb for himself, ordered it rebuilt and sponsored a design contest. Bramante won with his plan incorporating a Greek cross and a large dome. After Bramante's death in 1514, Michelangelo worked on the design at the Pope's bidding. Maderno extended the nave arm of the cross to make St Peter's into a Latin cross. Bernini added the finishing touch with a rounded colonnade that surrounds the piazza in front of St Peter's. Funds for such an ambitious building project were difficult to come by and resulted in the sale of indulgences, which was famously rejected in 1517 by Martin Luther in his Ninety-Five Theses on the Power and Efficacy of Indulgences and proved to be the initial catalyst for the Protestant Reformation. The basilica itself is a masterpiece of Renaissance architecture, filled with both Renaissance and Baroque paintings and sculpture. It is one of the four papal basilicas of Rome, along with the Basilica of St John Lateran, Basilica of Santa Maria Maggiore and the Basilica of St Paul Outside the Walls. Popes frequently preside over services at St Peter's because of its enormous capacity – it can accommodate 60,000 faithful under its roof.

# Papetoai Protestant Temple

1822–27 CE **Moorea, French Polynesia**

**COMMISSIONED BY** Pomare III of Tahiti  **MATERIALS** Wood, stucco, white hewn heron coral  **DIMENSIONS** 22 x 22 m/72 x 72 ft

**Basilica of San Vitale**

Papetoai's octagonal shape draws on a long Christian tradition of similarly shaped churches, such as the Basilica of San Vitale at Ravenna in Italy. Built between 526 and 548, San Vitale was commissioned by Emperor Justinian I. The basilica is an important example of early Christian Byzantine architecture and is particularly renowned for its magnificent mosaics.

'Places now used for worship in the islands, although not so numerous as formerly, are much more convenient and substantial.'

WILLIAM ELLIS, MISSIONARY

In 1808, Pomare, a Tahitian king, and all the Protestant missionaries in the kingdom were expelled and spent their exile in Papetoai, on the northern coast of nearby Moorea. There, Pomare expressed his desire to convert to Christianity and to build a church. He decided to build it in the native style, despite being counselled against doing so. He was called back to Tahiti in 1812 and the combination church-school that was originally built at Papetoai was an impermanent thatched-roof structure. This was replaced in the 1820s with a permanent structure that conformed more with the wishes of the missionaries. Also known as the Octagonal Church because of its shape, it was built, almost certainly intentionally, on the site of the Taputaputuatea marae (communal or sacred place). While marae are still in use in New Zealand, those in the South Pacific were abandoned or built over when the indigenous population converted to Christianity. One of the original stone spikes of the Taputaputuatea marae still stands beside the church. While the building of the church on the marae site undoubtedly pleased the missionaries, it was allowed by the locals, according to the missionary writer William Ellis, because of the large number of conversions taking place, including Patii, the marae's priest. The Papetoai Protestant Temple was partially rebuilt in the late 19th century. Now known as the Ebenezer Church, it has become a tourist attraction and is still used for Sunday services. It is the oldest European building in the South Pacific.

# Mãe de Deus Church

1873 CE **Saligão, Goa, India**

**STYLE** Neo-Gothic **FIRST STONE LAID** 7 February 1867
**AFFILIATION** Roman Catholic **MATERIALS** Stone, aqua tiles

Goa, India's smallest state, was under Portuguese control from 1510 until 1961. This 450-year period gave Goa a long Christian history. Nevertheless, in 1862 the village of Saligão still had only a small chapel and Archbishop João Crisóstomo de Amorim Pessoa suggested they consider building their own church. The church was built with stones from a demolished chapel – an abandoned Franciscan friary in Daugim – and freshly quarried stones, and was made the parish church of the newly created Parish of Saligão in 1873. It was named Mãe de Deus Church after the friary in Daugim and its main altar displays a famous wooden statue of the Mãe de Deus, or mother of God, from the friary that was transported to Saligão via an elaborate procession. The style of the church is neo-Gothic, which is typical of Raj architecture in areas of British-controlled India such as Mumbai, but not for Goa. The Goan interpretation of Gothic style contains many of the expected elements, such as buttresses with tall, pointed finials and thin, arched lancet windows on the sides. However, Mãe de Deus Church lacks the heaviness of most of the British neo-Gothic architecture found in India, with its open 'dome' on the bell tower, its white exterior, red roof and two levels of battens that shade each lancet window. The church is illuminated at night, which highlights the immaculate white exterior. The interior is also light and airy with pale gold arches, and elaborate gold and blue altars. There are also uniquely Goan touches, such as the local aqua tilework on the lower interior walls. Mãe de Deus is still in use today as a parish church.

## Christ Church

Nestled in the foothills of the Himalayas at Shimla, Christ Church is a fine example of the English neo-Gothic style in an area of India known as 'little England'. Built from 1844 to 1857, the church was designed more to evoke memories of home than to integrate local architectural traditions.

'The churches and convents of Goa, the former capital of the Portuguese Indies... illustrate the evangelization of Asia.'

UNESCO

## Santa Eulàlia Cathedral

Santa Eulàlia is the 14th-century Gothic cathedral of Barcelona, dedicated to a patron saint of the city who was martyred in Roman times. A view of the ceiling of Santa Eulàlia illustrates the influence Gothic architecture had on Antoni Gaudí, with its soaring columns and beautifully segmented geometric vaulting. A comparison also emphasizes the originality of Gaudí's organic forms at Sagrada Família.

'The expiatory church of La Sagrada Família is made by the people and is mirrored in them. It is a work that is in the hands of God and the will of the people.'

ANTONI GAUDÍ

# Sagrada Família

1882 CE **Barcelona, Spain**

**PRIMARY ARCHITECT** Antoni Gaudí    **CURRENT HEIGHT** 100 m/328 ft
**ESTIMATED FINAL HEIGHT** 170 m/558 ft    **COMPLETION DATE** 2026

Sagrada Família is an expiatory church, meaning it is being constructed entirely from donations from a campaign initially organized in 1866 by Devotees of Joseph. The original plans soon changed when modernist Catalan architect Antoni Gaudí took over the construction a year after it had begun. Gaudí oversaw the building of the crypt, apse, cloister and the Nativity facade before he was hit by a streetcar in 1926 and died. Fortunately, Gaudí had focused exclusively on the design of the church for a decade and left behind extensive models and drawings, as well as a crew of men who had shared in his vision. This vision includes a church complete with twelve towers symbolizing the Apostles and the highest central tower symbolizing Christ, which is to be surrounded by four shorter towers symbolizing the four Evangelists, and a smaller one for Mary. In the nave the columns demonstrate Gaudí's tendency to play with geometry, taking a twisting form that goes through a series of shapes from polygons at the bottom, to circles at the top. Gaudí introduced a sense of the outdoors into the structure. The columns symbolize trees, with branches that reach up and into the canopy of the ceiling. Two of the columns fancifully rest on two animals, a turtle and a tortoise, to represent the sea and the earth. Although the church remains incomplete, it continues to attract thousands of visitors and it was designated a UNESCO World Heritage Site in July 2005. In 2010 Pope Benedict XVI consecrated the church and proclaimed it a minor basilica (as distinct from a cathedral, which must be the seat of a bishop).

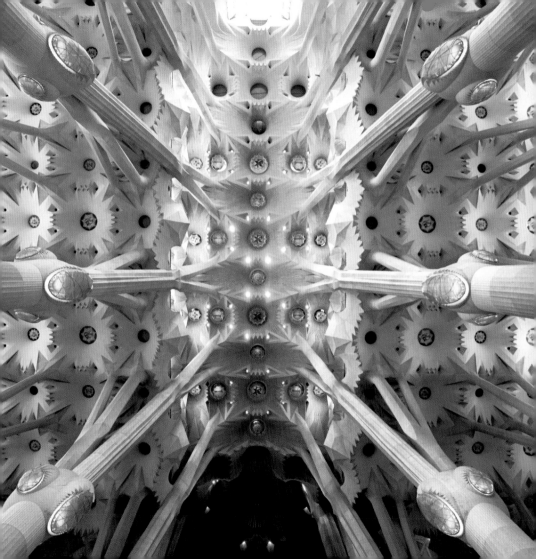

# Las Lajas Sanctuary

1916–49 CE **Nariño, Colombia**

**ARCHITECT** J. Gualberto Pérez, Lucindo Espinosa  **MATERIALS** Stone, brick
**TOWER HEIGHT** 100 m/328 ft  **DIMENSIONS** 27.5 x 15 m/90 x 49 ft

## Our Lady of Lourdes

A Marian apparition is an appearance by the Blessed Virgin Mary. Apparitions of Mary have also taken place in Europe, most famously when she appeared to fourteen-year-old Bernadette Soubirous in the cave of Massabielle, near Lourdes in south-western France in 1858. These apparitions are known as Our Lady of Lourdes and the grotto where she appeared receives millions of visitors a year who seek healing from the Lourdes water spring.

'The Lady, whom we venerate, is garbed as she was for the Conception, appeared in a *laja* [slab].'

FATHER JUAN DE SANTA GERTRUDIS, 18TH CENTURY

The Sanctuary of Las Lajas, in south-eastern Colombia, near the border with Ecuador, is built on the site where a miraculous apparition of the Virgin Mary took place. In 1754 an indigenous woman named Maria Mueces and her daughter Rosa were travelling and sought shelter from a storm under an outcrop in a canyon wall above the Guáitara River. Rosa, who was deaf and had never before spoken, suddenly cried out and pointed to an image of the Virgin on the canyon wall. The image quickly began attracting pilgrims, despite being far from any cities or important routes. A makeshift wooden chapel was built to house the image; it was later replaced with a small stone church. Today's building is much grander: it was built in the Gothic Revival style, complete with pointed arches, flying buttresses and rose windows. The impressive bridge spanning the river and taking full advantage of the sanctuary's location and waterfall views, was not added until the most recent church was built from 1916 to 1949. The cost of building it was raised entirely by donations. The veracity of the Virgin's apparition was confirmed by Pope Pius II in 1954, the same year he gave Las Lajas Sanctuary the title of basilica minor. The importance of Las Lajas was further underscored when it was declared part of the national patrimony by the Colombian government in 1984. The sanctuary is open to pilgrims and visitors throughout the year, but experiences increased religious visitors, especially from Ecuador and Colombia, in September on its patron feast days, at Christmas and the surrounding holy days and on Holy Thursday before Easter.

# Hallgrímskirkja

1945–86 CE **Reykjavik, Iceland**

**COMMISSIONED** 1937 **CONSECRATED** 1986 **ARCHITECT** Guðjón
Samúelsson **MATERIAL** Granite **HEIGHT** 74.5 m/244 ft

### 'Come to Me' Door

A recent addition to the church
is the 'Come to Me' bronze
door, which was designed by
Icelandic artist Leifur Breidfjord
and installed on the church's 25th
anniversary in 2010.

'It is a perfect expression
of the yearning of
Icelandic architects in
this period to find a new
architecture with "a native
character and in harmony
with the landscape".'

ARCHITECTURE.COM

The Church of Hallgrímur (or the Hallgrímskirkja) is the Lutheran
Parish Church for Reykjavik. It is one of several Icelandic churches
named for Hallgrímur Pétursson, a 17th-century poet and
clergyman, most famous for the *Passion Hymns*. The imposing bell
tower has a viewing platform and holds three bells to represent
Hallgrímur, his wife and their daughter. The Hallgrímskirkja's
imposing site, overlooking the centre of old Reykjavik, was set
aside in the early 20th century for a church to serve the growing
population of Iceland's largest city. The state architect, Guðjón
Samúelsson, was commissioned to design it in 1937 and work
began shortly after World War II. His design was controversial, but
his goal was to create a national Icelandic architecture based on
its unique geology. The basalt columns formed by cooling lava in
places such as Svartifoss were his main inspiration, although other
features such as the white glaciers of the island are also mimicked.
The Hallgrímskirkja is considered the pinnacle of Samúelsson's
career and his nationalist style. As a small family firm was used,
the construction process took more than forty years to complete,
with the architect not living to see its completion. Although the
interior is almost ascetically plain, it features a large pipe organ
by the German organ builder Johannes Klais, completed in 1992,
which is 15 metres (49 ft) high, weighs 25 tons and has 5,275 pipes
designed to fill the church with sound. It is the largest church in
Iceland, seating 1,200 people, and is one of the tallest structures in
the country. The church also has an observation tower and visitors
can take a lift up to the viewing deck.

# Thorncrown Chapel

1979–80 CE  **Eureka Springs, Arkansas, USA**

**STYLE** Modern   **ARCHITECT** E. Fay Jones   **MATERIALS** Glass, wood, stone
**DIMENSIONS** 7 x 12 x 14.5 m/23 x 39 x 48 ft   **AREA** 3.1 hectares/7.6 ac.

Arkansas schoolteacher Jim Reed had intended to build a house
for his retirement on land that he owned in the Ozark Mountains.
However, he decided to share the inspiring views there by building
a small chapel and he hired architect E. Fay Jones to design it.
Jones was a student of Frank Lloyd Wright and the Prairie School
of architecture, and his work maintained Wright's principle to
make a building belong to the space that it occupies. With 425
windows, more than 550 square metres (6,000 sq ft) of glass,
its base of more than 100 tons of native stone and flagstone,
and wooden beams, Jones successfully integrated Thorncrown
Chapel into the woods and vistas surrounding it. In part, this was
achieved by using only materials indigenous to north-western
Arkansas that could be carried by two men through the woods
to the site. Indeed, he was so successful that the chapel received
the American Institute of Architects design of the year award, as
well as their decade and twenty-five year awards. Furthermore,
the building was added to the National Register of Historic Places
in 2000, an honour granted to places younger than fifty years old
only when they are considered exceptional. Jones himself thought
of his work as inspired by Gothic church architecture in Europe,
particularly Sainte-Chapelle in Paris. The small, intimate scale of
both chapels, their abundance of windows and light, and their
soaring heights illustrate this similarity, despite Thorncrown's
strict modernism. The acclaim the chapel has received is not
simply professional, but public, with more than 250,000 people
visiting a year, three weddings a day and services held each Sunday.

## United States Air Force Academy Cadet Chapel

Another famous modern church
is the Cadet Chapel of the United
States Air Force Academy. More
than 46 m (150 ft) tall, it has
dedicated areas of worship for
Protestants, Catholics, Jews and
Buddhists, as well as an all-faith
room for others. Architect Walter
A. Netsch was closely linked with
the Brutalist style, which focused
on massive, rugged structures.

'This small elegant chapel
in the woods, with its
lacework of trusses, is a
metaphor for its place –
a forest within a forest.'

MICHAEL COCKRAM,
ARCHITECTURE WRITER

# Church of the Light

1989 CE **Ibaraki, Osaka Prefecture, Japan**

**ARCHITECT** Tadao Ando    **AFFILIATION** United Church of Christ in Japan
**MATERIALS** Reinforced concrete, wood    **AREA** 113 sq m/1,216 sq ft

The Church of the Light is a functioning church belonging to
the United Church of Christ, the largest Protestant denomination
in Japan. When Japanese architect Tadao Ando was hired to
design and build the chapel, he had to create it as an annex to
the existing minister's residence and wooden church. Ando, who
works in a minimalist modern style, created a simple structure
with its width and length forming a 1:3 ratio. He also carefully
and thoughtfully controlled the entry to the chapel by introducing
a wall that unequally bisects the chapel at a 15° angle. This creates
a small room in the shape of a right-angled triangle that serves
as the entry. Access to the worship space is only achieved by
slipping through where the bisecting wall does not completely
meet the chapel wall. The construction of the walls, while using
the most utilitarian materials, was made with precision by
master craftsmen. The reinforced concrete shell is 38 cm (15 in)
thick. Benches and floorboards in the church were made out of
scaffolding used during the building's construction. The focus
of the austere, undecorated chapel is the east wall, which allows
the morning light to enter through a cross-shaped opening.
Playing with light is one of the enduring themes of Ando's work,
and here the incoming light has the ability to make it seem as
if the wall is dissolving. While the church echoes aspects of
traditional Japanese aesthetics, such as simplicity and *kire* (cutting,
part of the opposing forces of cutting and continuation), it also
reveals Ando's international influences, such as the emphasis on
boldness instead of subtlety.

## Church on the Water

Although Tadao Ando has mainly
designed private residences and
museums, he also created the
Church on the Water in Hokkaido.
Again, this building plays with a
dissolving wall, but differently, as
here the front glass wall looks out
over the water.

'Light gives, with each
moment, new form
to being and new
interrelationships to
things, and architecture
condenses light to its
most concise being.
The creation of space
in architecture is simply
the condensation and
purification of the
power of light.'

TADAO ANDO

# 2

## Places of Contemplation

## Moses

Moses, seen here in a sculpture by Michelangelo, is one of the most important prophets in Judaism, Christianity and Islam. His deeds, such as freeing the Israelites from Egypt and receiving the Ten Commandments, are told in the Torah, Old Testament and Qur'an.

'Far into the vast and inhospitable wilderness of biblical renown, it dawns upon the weary traveller and adventurer as a haven of peace and a hospitable refuge.'

AZIZ S. ATIYA,
COPTIC HISTORIAN
AND ISLAMIC SCHOLAR

# St Catherine's Monastery

c. 548–65 CE **Sinai, Egypt**

**COMMISSIONED BY** Emperor Justinian I  **ARCHITECTS** Stephanos and others
**AFFILIATION** Greek [Eastern] Orthodox  **MATERIAL** Dressed granite

St Catherine's Monastery (officially named the Sacred Monastery of the God-Trodden Mount Sinai) in Egypt is the oldest Christian monastery still in use for its initial function. However, its location at the foot of Mount Horeb, where, according to the Old Testament, Moses received the Ten Commandments from God, makes it a sacred place for all three monotheistic religions. In the 4th century, St Helena, Constantine the Great's mother, ordered that a small Chapel of the Burning Bush be built around the site where God appeared to Moses. Later, Emperor Justinian I sent teams of men to build the walls to enclose the chapel for the dual purpose of providing protection for the monks living in Sinai and securing the road from the port of Aqaba to Suez. Since at least 384, the Sinai desert had been a popular area for anchorites, the first monks, who spent their lives alone in the deserts of Egypt and Syria in imitation of Christ's time in the wilderness. Then, in the 6th century, anchorites were consolidated into communal monastic foundations. The main building of St Catherine's is the Church of the Transfiguration, which was designed by Stephanos, built in the 560s and was dedicated to the Virgin Mary. When the remains of St Catherine of Alexandria, a 3rd-century martyr, were found in c. 800, her head and hand were revered as relics and the dedication was changed. More than 170 Sinai saints are honoured by the church in addition to St Catherine. Numerous additions and small restorations have occurred over the years, including the north wall being damaged during Napoleon's campaign in 1801. St Catherine's Monastery is a UNESCO World Heritage Site.

# Coldingham Priory

c. 640 CE **Berwickshire, Scotland, UK**

**FOUNDED BY** St Aebbe the Elder  **SECOND PRIORY FOUNDED** 1098
**VICTORIAN RENOVATION** 1855  **MATERIAL** Stone

Coldingham Priory was first established in the 6th century by
St Aebbe the Elder, a Northumbrian queen. Fleeing her second
husband, Aebbe retreated to the defensible dower lands from
her first marriage and established a monastery at Coldingham,
on the modern border between England and Scotland. The
original Coldingham was a 'double house', meaning that it took
both men and women and was ruled by an abbess, in this case
Aebbe. Coldingham was also affiliated with the Columban order
of monks from Ireland instead of the Benedictine order from
Rome. However, the first Coldingham was short-lived and it
burned down in 683. St Bede famously attributed the fire to God's
judgement upon the sinful activities of many of the monks and
nuns who did not follow Aebbe's holy example. Coldingham was
rebuilt in the 12th century by Benedictine monks, beginning
with King Edgar of Scotland giving permission to build a priory
church in 1098. At its height, Coldingham was a centre of Scottish
monasticism and comprised the church, a cloister, a graveyard, a
chapter house and a refectory/hospicium. However, this version
also saw destructive events, including a raid by King John of
England and an episode in 1420 in which prior William Drax
smoked out some border raiders and lost control of the priory to
the Scottish king. The worst blow struck when Oliver Cromwell
had it bombarded in 1648 to flush out Royalists and most of
the buildings were destroyed. The choir wall of the church still
stands, and was used to build a Victorian parish church in 1855,
which is still in use today by the Church of Scotland.

### St Aebbe the Elder

St Aebbe, a Northumbrian
princess and queen, was
not unusual in her role as a
the founder of a monastery.
Throughout Gaul and England,
the conversion of Germanic
kings and nobles soon saw a
large number of royals founding
monasteries and then ruling them
as abbesses and abbots.

'The time is at hand
when a devouring fire
shall reduce to ashes all
the buildings which you
here behold, both public
and private.'

ST ADOMNÁN'S PROPHECY
ABOUT COLDINGHAM,
AS TOLD BY BEDE

# Mont Saint-Michel

709 CE **Normandy, France**

**FOUNDED BY** Bishop Aubert   **ARCHITECT** William de Volpiano
**CIRCUMFERENCE** 960 m/3,150 ft   **AREA** 100 hectares/247 ac.

## St Michael's Mount

The daughter house of St Michael's of Penzance is also dedicated to the Archangel Michael, who is celebrated in Judaism, Christianity and Islam. Within Christianity, he plays an important role in the New Testament Book of Revelation, leading God's armies against Satan and defeating him.

'One needs to be eight centuries old to know what this mass of encrusted architecture meant to its builders.'

HENRY ADAMS, AUTHOR

The monastery of Mont Saint-Michel is built upon a tidal island, only accessible via a causeway from the mainland coast. Its foundation occurred when Aubert, Bishop of Avranches, was ordered by the Archangel Michael to build a church in 708. In the legend, Aubert declined the request until Michael used a finger to burn a hole in the bishop's skull. Aubert's church, a small pre-Romanesque oratory, tended by twelve men, was consecrated in 709. However, it was not made a monastery until William the Conqueror, as a reward for loyalty, transferred the Benedictine commune from St Wandrille Abbey and placed Abbot Maynard in charge of building. It was also awarded a small Cornish island that became a Norman daughter priory named St Michael's Mount of Penzance. Most visible at the highest point of the island is the Romanesque church, built upon the very top of the mount, and requiring a large number of crypts and chapels to support it. In the 13th century, King Philip Augustus added the Gothic 'Merveille' section that includes the cloister and the refectory. During the Middle Ages it remained an important pilgrimage site and the most important location dedicated to Michael. Thanks to swift tides and its reinforcing walls, Mont Saint-Michel successfully resisted siege during the Hundred Years War in the 14th and 15th centuries. During the French Revolution religious use ceased and it was turned into a prison. In 1966, on the 1,000th anniversary of the monastery, a small group of monks returned to the island. It was designated a UNESCO World Heritage Site in 1979 and welcomes more than three million visitors a year.

# Santa Maria of Montserrat Monastery

9th century CE **Catalonia, Spain**

**CONSECRATED** 1592  **MATERIALS** Stone, brick, marble
**DIMENSIONS** 68 x 21.5 x 33 m/224 x 70½ x 109 ft

Some 45 kilometres (28 miles) west of Barcelona lies the Santa Maria of Montserrat Monastery, whose name means 'serrated mountain' in Catalan. Its legendary origins tell a story of shepherds who saw visions and found an image of the Virgin Mary on a cave wall. A small chapel was built around the cave and by the end of the 9th century there were four small chapels, of which only St Iscle still exists. In the late 12th century, the wooden black madonna of Montserrat (La Moreneta) was sculpted and soon became the source of its own legends, including monks building their monastery around it because they were miraculously unable to move it. The Gothic cloister, now in ruins, was built in 1476 and was followed by the basilica in the 16th century. Much of the monastery was destroyed during the Napoleonic wars, when it was robbed of most of its treasures and left abandoned, only to be rebuilt in the late 19th and early 20th centuries. The basilica's facade was rebuilt in a neo-Renaissance style in 1901 to match the style of the Renaissance interior. Agapit and Venanci Vallmitjana sculpted the figures of Christ and the Twelve Apostles that overlook the marble-floored atrium. The monastery is a symbol of Catalonian identity, in part because of a Mass that was held there in 1947, attended by 100,000 people and with prayers said in Catalan, a language forbidden by Francisco Franco. During Franco's rule, the monastery became a sanctuary for political dissidents. Today it is home to 100 Benedictine monks.

## La Moreneta

It was in front of La Moreneta that the soldier Ignatius of Loyola laid down his arms in 1522 and devoted his life to asceticism. He went on to found the Society of Jesus, or Jesuits, and was later canonized.

'We can say that the precious stone that adorns and embellishes Catalonia is the mountain of Montserrat.'

JERONI PUJADES, HISTORIAN

# Cluny Abbey

910 CE **Burgundy, France**

**STYLE** Romanesque **DEDICATED BY** Pope Innocent II in 1130
**MATERIALS** Stone, glass **LENGTH** 187 m/613 ft (Cluny III)

The abbey at Cluny was founded by William I, Duke of Aquitaine in 909. Although Cluny, like nearly all the Roman Catholic monasteries of its day, followed the Rule of St Benedict, Duke William granted it a new and unique freedom from the influence of local lords or bishops. This meant that the community was answerable only to St Peter and, by extension, to the Pope in Rome as his earthly successor. This influential monastery also brought in a new liturgy that was devoted almost entirely to prayer, including elaborate Masses for the dead, and nobles and kings made enormous gifts to ensure their names were incorporated. It was also at Cluny that the idea of a daughter house was introduced: instead of each monastery being independent, a network of affiliated Cluniac monasteries was established across western Europe, known as priories instead of abbeys, which owed loyalty to the mother house. Cluny was viewed as the leader of Western monasticism through to the early 12th century. The original abbey church, Cluny I, and a second church built in c. 970 were too small to hold the community of more than 300 monks. A new Romanesque church, known as Cluny III, was finished in the mid-12th century and was the largest church in the West until modern St Peter's was completed in Rome in 1626. Today only the southern of the two original transepts survives, as the rest of the church was torn down during the French Revolution. Nonetheless, its use of flying buttresses and a recessed portal on the main facade influenced the development of French Gothic architecture as much as its monks influenced monasticism.

## St Benedict of Nursia

In the early 5th century, St Benedict of Nursia wrote a book of precepts that guided monks living communally with moderation and devotion. Known as St Benedict's Rule, it dominated Roman Catholic monasteries until the 13th century.

'I...while I am still able, have considered it advisable – nay, most necessary, that from the temporal goods which have been conferred upon me I should give some little portion for the gain of my soul.'

WILLIAM OF AQUITAINE, FOUNDATION CHARTER OF CLUNY

# Round Tower

11th century CE  **Glendalough, County Wicklow, Ireland**

**FOUNDED BY** St Kevin  **MATERIALS** Mica slate, granite
**DIMENSIONS** 5 x 30 m/16 x 100 ft

### Monastery Gateway

Glendalough's many buildings were enclosed by a wall and entry was controlled through a granite gateway. It is the only surviving gate of this style in Ireland; it was originally two storeys with a gatekeeper's lodgings above and a timber roof.

'The round tower – tall, delicately tapering, smartly capped by a conical stone roof – is the most poetic of the Celtic architectural creations. No towers are more graceful than these upward-pointing stone fingers of Ireland.'

KENNETH JOHN CONANT, AUTHOR

The Round Tower at Glendalough stands in a much older monastic complex famously founded by St Kevin in the 6th century. Like the desert monks, early Irish monks most often sought a solitary existence, and Kevin found his in Glendalough (meaning 'glen of two lakes'), in a small cave overlooking the valley. As his reputation grew, others flocked to join him until the monastic community reached 1,000 monks, with a total population of 4,000 at its height several centuries later. Among the many churches, dormitories, scriptoria, guest houses and other buildings is a beautiful example of an Irish *cloigtheach* (bell house). While many have imagined these towers to have been defensive refuges from Viking raids, or watchtowers, this has been disproved, in part because the Viking raids began in the area in *c.* 800 and the tower was not built for at least another 200 years. Furthermore, while ladders were used to go between the five storeys inside the building, archaeological evidence shows that there were originally stairs leading to the raised doorway instead of retractable ladders for defence. Instead, these Irish towers were laid out with their doorways facing the main church and used as the bell towers their names imply and as landmarks for approaching visitors. The Glendalough Round Tower stayed in use until the monastery was partially destroyed by English troops in 1398, although it continued in use as a church. The conical roof was rebuilt in 1876 using the original bricks that were found inside the tower, but it is otherwise intact and still draws in hundreds of thousands of tourists and pilgrims each year.

# St Michael's Golden-Domed Monastery

1108, REBUILT 1999 CE  **Kiev, Ukraine**

**AFFILIATION** Ukrainian Orthodox **BELL TOWER HEIGHT** 46 m/151 ft
**ARCHITECTS** I. Melnyk, A. Zayika, V. Korol

### Eucharist Mosaic

One of the original mosaics from St Michael's, now preserved in Kiev's St Sophia Cathedral, depicts the Eucharist, or Last Supper, in which Jesus told his disciples to break bread and drink wine in remembrance of him. It is the root of the central Christian rite of Eucharist or Communion.

'Let everyone make their contribution to this holy matter, which will become the symbol of national unity among all the [government] branches of power, churches, entrepreneurs, bankers, regular citizens — a union of all Ukrainians of the world.'

PRESIDENT LEONID KUCHMA

The reconstruction of St Michael's Golden-Domed Monastery in Kiev was part of an attempt to reclaim the national and cultural Ukrainian heritage after the fall of the Soviet Union. In the 1930s the Soviets declared that, because the original medieval church of the monastery built by the Kievan Rus prince Sviatopolk II Iziaslavych had been redone in the Ukrainian Baroque style, it was no longer of historical or artistic value. Despite the protest of Professor Mykola Makarenko, who refused to sign the demolition act and later died in a Soviet prison, the church and the 18th-century Economic Gates and bell tower were demolished. Only the refectory dating from 1713 survived because it was used as changing rooms for a nearby sports complex. Fortunately a team was allowed to remove many of the 12th-century Byzantine style mosaics before the demolition. As early as the 1970s, there were calls for St Michael's to be rebuilt, however, it was not until after the collapse of the Soviet Union in the 1990s that the plans were put into action. The reconstruction, which used many old building techniques, recovered more than 260 artefacts and revealed the intact base of the original church, which is visible today in the rebuilt crypt. The sky-blue church exterior was rebuilt with seven pear-shaped golden domes in the more moderately ornamental Ukrainian Baroque style, with slightly cleaner lines than its Western counterpart. St Michael's is once more a functioning monastery, with a museum in the rebuilt bell tower.

# Tintern Abbey

1131 CE **Monmouthshire, Wales, UK**

**STYLE** Gothic   **FOUNDED BY** Walter de Clare, Lord of Chepstow
**ABBEY CHURCH LENGTH** 72 m/236 ft   **MATERIAL** Sandstone

## Gisborough Priory

Although many churches continued to be used for Anglican services during the reign of Henry VIII, others, especially those associated with the newly forbidden monasteries, either fell into ruin or were refitted for secular purposes. Gisborough is a ruined Augustinian priory in North Yorkshire, England that was founded in 1119. The Romanesque Norman priory was largely destroyed by fire in 1289, but was rebuilt over the next century on a grander scale and in the Gothic style.

'So sad, so fresh, the days that are no more.'

ALFRED, LORD TENNYSON, 'TEARS, IDLE TEARS'

Tintern Abbey represents the spread of the Cistercian monks from France to the rest of Western Europe. It was the first Cistercian monastery in Wales and, like all Cistercian houses, it followed the Benedictine rule. Cistercians sought to reform the way in which the Rule of Benedict was implemented by emphasizing a form of monasticism with more physical work, white robes instead of black and less elaborate churches and monasteries. Tintern Abbey was largely patronized by the Lords of Chepstow, including Walter de Clare who had helped to found the first English Cistercian house in Waverley in 1128. For Tintern, de Clare brought monks from the Cistercian house of L'Aumône in Blois, France. The monastery was later rebuilt by another Lord Chepstow, Roger Bigod, in the 13th century, but after the Black Death the Cistercians began having trouble recruiting lay brothers to work the farmlands and had to tenant out the granges instead. The monastery encountered financial trouble when many of its properties were destroyed by Welsh rebels in the early 15th century. In 1536, Abbot Wyche surrendered the abbey and all its estates to King Henry VIII during the Dissolution of the Monasteries; the buildings and grounds soon fell into ruin. However, in its derelict state, Tintern Abbey found a new life as inspiration for Romantic poets and artists. Its green grass floor and ceiling open to the sky inspired works such as poet William Wordsworth's 'Lines Composed a Few Miles Above Tintern Abbey' (1798) and Alfred, Lord Tennyson's 'Tears, Idle Tears' (1847). The ruins were also famously painted by J. M. W. Turner.

# Krak des Chevaliers

C. 1140–70 CE  **Tartus, Syria**

**FOUNDED BY** Knights Hospitaller  **MATERIALS** Limestone, ashlar facing
**OUTER WALL HEIGHT** 9 m/30 ft  **AREA** 2.6 hectares/6.4 ac.

Krak des Chevaliers is a fortified monastery or medieval castle built by the Knights Hospitaller during the Crusades. It sits on a high hilltop east of Tartus in Syria. When the first Crusaders passed through in 1099 the site was occupied by Kurds, but it soon came under Crusader control and was given by Raymond II, Count of Tripoli to the Hospitallers. First formed to assist religious pilgrims from Europe, the Knights Hospitaller served a dual purpose: to offer aid and give military protection to the Crusader County of Tripoli. In order to perform both these duties, starting in the 1140s the Hospitallers built a castle they called 'Crac de l'Ospital', which they later rebuilt after an earthquake in 1170. It was this rebuilding that gave the structure its current form of a concentric castle, meaning that it has two sets of curtain walls, with the interior being taller for defence purposes. It is also regarded as a spur castle because of its construction on an already defensible point. During its golden age in the first half of the 13th century, Krak des Chevaliers was an administrative centre collecting taxes, as well as hosting a large garrison of 2,000 men and controlling the surrounding countryside along the road between Tripoli and Homs. As Hospitaller power diminished, the Mamluk Sultan Baibars I captured the fortress after a thirty-six-day siege in 1271. Largely forgotten by Europeans, it was rediscovered and given its current name in the late 19th century. Krak des Chevaliers was designated a UNESCO World Heritage Site in 2006, but it has suffered significant damage during the recent Syrian civil war, both to its walls and to its interior architectural features.

## Crusader Cross

Jerusalem had always been a place of pilgrimage for Christians, but beginning in 1096 Europeans began going on armed pilgrimages, known as Crusades. Those who vowed to make this pilgrimage were said to have 'taken the cross' and were identified by the Crusader cross, such as the one on the coat of arms worn by Godfrey of Bouillon, who helped to lead the First Crusade (1096–99).

'Perhaps the best preserved and most wholly admirable castle in the world.'

T. E. LAWRENCE, SOLDIER

# Convent of St Agnes of Bohemia

1231–34 CE **Prague, Czech Republic**

**STYLE** French Gothic    **FOUNDED BY** King Wenceslas I
**MATERIALS** Grey brick, sandstone    **HIGHEST POINT** 37 m/121 ft

## St Clare of Assisi

St Clare of Assisi, who founded the Poor Clares and wrote their rule of life, corresponded regularly with St Agnes. This correspondence linked the Bohemian royal house and the popes, but it also offered a more personal connection to two women who were limited in their desire to serve God and the poor because, as women, they were required to be cloistered.

'And I beseech you all, my ladies, and counsel you, to live always in this most holy life and poverty.'

ST FRANCIS TO ST CLARE

After a failed engagement to a German prince, Princess Agnes of Bohemia refused further engagements, instead choosing to focus her life on religious poverty and service. She became involved in helping her brother, King Wenceslas I, establish the first Franciscan monastery in Bohemia. The Franciscans were a new order of mendicant preachers, only a few decades old, and their fresh ideas of ministering to the urban poor resonated with Agnes who often tended the sick, including lepers. When she learned of their companion female order established by St Francis of Assisi and St Clare, the Poor Clares, Agnes soon founded the first house of Clares north of the Alps in Prague. She served there as abbess until the end of her life in 1282. The complex originally included a church that was dedicated to St Francis in 1234, which is the oldest building. The St Salvator Church, built between 1270 and 1280, became the burial place of the Bohemian royalty, including Agnes' father, Ottokar I of Bohemia, her brother, and even Agnes herself. Architecturally, with the convent the builders created the first example of the French Gothic style in Prague or even Bohemia. The Hussite (or Bohemian) wars of the 15th century, the eviction of the Poor Clares in favour of the Dominicans in 1556 and a fire in 1689 left the convent only partly rebuilt until it was dissolved by Emperor Josef II in 1782. Since being restored in the 20th century, it is today a museum of medieval art run by the Czech National Gallery.

# Simonopetra Monastery

1257 CE (REBUILT 1581, 1626, 1891) **Mount Athos, Greece**

**AFFILIATION** Eastern Orthodox   **FOUNDED BY** Simon the Athonite
**FEAST** The Nativity of Christ   **MATERIAL** Carved rock

The Holy Monastery of Simonos Petra (or Simonopetra) was founded by a Greek Orthodox saint, Simon the Athonite, in the 13th century after Simon had a dream in which the Theotokos (Mary) told him to build a monastery upon the rock and promised she would protect it. Simon did as she asked, naming the original monastery 'New Bethlehem' in celebration of the Nativity. The original monastery went through a cycle of rebuilding, including expansion in the 14th century, and was rebuilt after fires in 1581, 1626 and 1891. The current form is from the rebuilding after 1891 that was largely funded by Russian sources. By 1973 the monastery was largely abandoned until it was repopulated by monks from nearby Metéora. Today there are approximately sixty monks and Simonopetra is renowned for its choir's maintenance of the Byzantine musical chant tradition, especially 'Agni Parthene' (O Virgin Pure). Mount Athos, a remote, mountainous peninsula in north-eastern Greece, was made a UNESCO World Heritage Site in 1988 because of its twenty working Greek Orthodox monasteries housing 1,400 monks. First settled by ascetics in the 9th century, Mount Athos was allowed to develop into a monastic republic by an imperial chrysobull from Basil I the Macedonian in 883. Known for its monastic communities, Mount Athos is forbidden to women and children to encourage celibacy. The layout of the Athonite monasteries influenced those of Orthodox monasteries as far away as Russia. This includes a rectangular fortification with towers at the corner, an unattached church in the centre and specific areas reserved for communal purposes and for defence.

### Cloister

Although Mount Athos forbids women in order to encourage celibacy, the Eastern Orthodox Church accepts married priests. Unlike the Roman Catholic Church, where all clergy must be unmarried, Eastern Orthodox priests may be ordained even if they are already married.

'Assist me and deliver me/ protect me from the enemy. And make me an inheritor/of blessed life eternal.'

'AGNI PARTHENE', BYZANTINE CHANT

## St Simeon Stylites

The pillar-tops at Metéora offered protection and enough space to build small monasteries, but the location also mimicked the life of St Simeon Stylites. Simeon was a 5th-century Syrian saint who lived for more than thirty years on a platform on top of a pillar. He attracted much interest and many imitators, but also showed so much humility that the emperor begged him to come down and see a doctor when he was ill. He refused and was cured by God.

'Partake of the sacred mysteries, according to the tradition of the Fathers and of the great Basil.'

CANONICAL RULE
OF ATHANASIOS

# Metéora

1356–72 CE **Kalambaka, Greece**

**AFFILIATION** Greek Orthodox **FOUNDED BY** Athanasios Koinovitis
**HIGHEST POINT** 615 m/2,017 ft above sea level

Metéora, meaning 'middle of the sky', is an Eastern Orthodox complex of six monasteries. The neighbouring caves have been occupied since at least 21,000 BCE, but the area in northern Greece was repurposed as a sacred Christian space in the 9th century CE when a group of hermit monks moved from the caves to the tops of the nearby natural sandstone rock pillars. In 1344 Athanasios Koinovitis arrived and by 1356 he began to build the first and largest monastery, Great Meteoron, transforming the hermitic life into a more communal one. In total, at least twenty-four monasteries were built, in part because of the religiously desirable isolation, but also because with only retractable ladders and nets giving access to people and goods, the monasteries were incredibly defensible from Turkish raids. Many were abandoned in the 17th century, leaving only six today: Great Meteoron, Varlaam, St Nicholas, St Stephen, the Holy Trinity and Rousanou (pictured here). By the 20th century, even these were in bad shape, none more so than the monastery of St Stephen, which was bombed during World War II and suffered further damage in the civil war that followed, when its frescoes were defaced by communist rebels. The remaining monasteries have been restored. Four are currently inhabited by monks and two by nuns, although their numbers have been as low as a single monk at St Nicholas. Great Meteoron is the highest existing monastery, but the monastery of Ypselotera used to stand on a higher neighbouring pinnacle, until it was abandoned in the 17th century and never restored. Metéora was declared a UNESCO World Heritage Site in 1988.

# Solovetsky Monastery

1436 CE **Solovetsky Islands, Russia**

**FOUNDED BY** Zosima   **MATERIALS** Brick, stone, boulders
**HIGHEST POINT** 11m/36ft   **WALL THICKNESS** 7m/23ft at base

### Iconostasis

One of the highlights of Solovetsky Cathedral is the six-tier iconostasis (icon screen). It is a reconstruction of the 16th-century iconostasis from the cathedral's side chapel that was taken with dissidents when they fled during the siege of 1668 and some of the panels were lost.

'Any Russian, just like any other person coming here, can stop for meditation and try to answer the most important question of all: what am I living for, and what do I need to do to make my life right?'

ARCHIMANDRITE PORPHYRY

Solovetsky Monastery, on the shores of the White Sea on one of the Solovetsky Islands, is less than 200 km (124 miles) from the Arctic Circle and extremely remote, even today. In 1429 two monks, Gherman and Savvatiy, arrived in this distant part of the Novgorod State, followed in 1436 by the first abbot, Zosima. A large donation of land in 1450 allowed the monastery to cover not only the six major islands of the archipelago, but also a part of the mainland. After control was passed to Moscow, it became a commercial centre and northern fortress as well, ruled by an archimandrite, a superior abbot appointed directly by a bishop, or in Solovetsky's case, by the tsar and the patriarch. Its role as a fortress saw it repel attacks from the Livonian Order of the Teutonic Knights, the Swedes and the English. However, during the Raskol, or schism, of the Russian Orthodox Church, Solovetsky sided with the Old Believers and resisted the reforms demanded by the tsar and Patriarch Nikon. After a siege lasting from 1668 to 1676, almost all 500 rebels died when a defecting monk showed the tsar's forces an unguarded window. Stalin turned Solovetsky into a prison and labour camp after the Revolution in 1917, and it became a prototype for the Gulag system. In 1990 a small brotherhood returned to the monastery and today it is also a museum. The complex was designated a UNESCO World Heritage Site in 1992. The central square contains the churches, refectory and bell tower, which were built in the Novgorod style, with square buildings topped by steep roofs and domes, as well as brick and rough stone covered in stucco and whitewashed.

# El Escorial

1563–84 CE **San Lorenzo de El Escorial, Spain**

**AFFILIATION** Roman Catholic   **ARCHITECT** Juan Bautista de Toledo
**DIMENSIONS** 224 x 153 m / 735 x 502 ft   **MATERIALS** Quarried grey granite

**Temptation of Christ**

One of the best-known scenes painted on the walls of El Escorial is the *Temptation of Christ* by Italian artist Pellegrino Tibaldi. This represents Jesus' test in the desert when he resisted Satan's offers of physical ease and worldly power.

'Simplicity in the construction, severity in the whole, nobility without arrogance, majesty without ostentation.'

KING PHILIP II OF SPAIN

El Escorial is a monastery, pantheon, basilica, convent, school, library and royal palace built by King Philip II of Spain. His reasons for building were as mixed as its uses: El Escorial commemorates the 1557 Spanish victory of the Battle of St Quentin; it provided a worthy burial place for his father, Holy Roman Emperor Charles V; and it provided support to the Counter-Reformation, a cause Philip II zealously supported. The complex was designed by Juan Bautista de Toledo, who had worked on the basilica of St Peter's in Rome. The influences on the design are equally diverse. The grill-like floor plan, with the basilica church at the centre and many courtyards, reflects the grill upon which St Lawrence, a Spanish-born martyr, was tortured and killed in the 3rd century. The design of the complex also reflects the Spanish courtyard tradition, as seen at Seville's Alcázar and Granada's Alhambra. Lastly, it is probable that Philip II had Flavius Josephus' account of the Temple of Solomon in Jerusalem in mind. The basilica shows a more definite influence on de Toledo from Michelangelo's original Greek cross-shaped design for St Peter's. Philip desired only the best available artists to work on the interior and the results are works by a veritable who's who of 16th-century artists, including Titian, Tintoretto, El Greco, Velázquez, Pellegrino Tibaldi, Paolo Veronese, Alonso Cano and José de Ribera. The Pantheon of Kings in the crypt below the royal chapel continues to be the burial place of Spanish kings and queens. A UNESCO World Heritage Site since 1984, El Escorial stands as perhaps the most important example of Spanish Renaissance architecture.

# Abbey of Our Lady of Nový Dvůr

2001 CE **Toužim, Czech Republic**

**CONSECRATED** 2004 **AREA OF ESTATE** 100 hectares/247 ac.
**ARCHITECT** John Pawson **MATERIALS** Plaster, concrete, glass, wood, stone

The Abbey of Our Lady of Nový Dvůr was the first monastery built in the Czech Republic after the Velvet Revolution of 1989 allowed the return of religious expression. A number of Czech men had joined the Trappist monastery of Sept-Fons Abbey in France and, nearly ten years later, it was decided to found a new daughter house in a remote area west of Prague. A large estate with a derelict 18th-century manor house was transformed into a working monastery. The Baroque manor house was renovated by Jan Soukup, and John Pawson designed three new wings to form the cloister around what had originally been the manor's courtyard. One of the great successes of the project is the way in which the modern and Baroque wings harmonize with one another, eliminating visual and functional distractions as Pawson intended. The Trappists are a 17th-century branch of the Cistercians, who follow the simple life of prayer and work advocated by St Bernard of Clairvaux. While emphatically modern, the monastery was built with the Cistercian focus on interior life in mind. One aspect of the monastery is without precedent, however: the cloister passageway ceilings are cantilevered, which frees them from the need for columns and allows the entire outer wall to be made of uninterrupted glass. The modern aesthetics of the abbey church are the backdrop for a traditional life that begins with services at 3:30 a.m. each morning. The church is open to visitors each morning for the 9:15 a.m. divine service.

### Calvin Klein Collections Store

The abbot of Sept-Fons was convinced to hire John Pawson based on photographs he had seen of the Calvin Klein Collections Store in New York City. Although an odd pairing at first glance, the minimalism of the store reflected traditional Cistercian building aesthetics.

'An absence of visual and functional distraction supports the goal of monastic life: concentration on God.'

JOHN PAWSON, ARCHITECT

3

Mosaics, Sculpture, Paintings and Glass

# Roman Wall Paintings

2nd–5th centuries CE **Catacombs of Priscilla, Rome, Italy**

**FOUNDED BY** St Priscilla   **ARTIST** Not known   **MATERIALS** Pigment and plaster on volcanic tufa   **TECHNIQUE** Fresco

## The Good Shepherd

The image of Christ as the Good Shepherd is typical of early Christian depictions, showing him as a young, slim, clean-shaven man. This was an acceptable Roman theme during a period when overt Christian iconography could be dangerous. It was also a symbol of Christ's humility and humanity, and his role in watching over his flock of believers as noted in John 10:11 when he says 'I am the good shepherd. The good shepherd lays down his life for the sheep.'

'St Priscilla, who devoted herself and her goods to the service of the martyrs.'

ENTRY FOR 16 JANUARY, *THE ROMAN MARTYROLOGY*

Roman burial required cremation and burial outside the city walls. However, early Christians, believing that the second coming of Christ was immediate and would necessitate a bodily resurrection, chose inhumation instead. It was difficult to find land in Rome, but a noblewoman named Priscilla, believed to be the wife of Manius Acilius Glabrio, a Roman consul in 91 CE, gave use of a quarry in honour of her martyred husband. This multi-levelled, 13-km (8-mile) network of passages is known as the 'Queen of Catacombs' because of the many popes and martyrs buried there. It is also famous for its beautiful wall frescoes, which provide the best source of early Christian art and iconography. The majority of the frescoes depict biblical scenes and early martyrs, but one of the most famous gives the Cubiculum of the Veiled Woman its name. Featuring a figure in a loose purple garment and a head covering, with her hands outstretched in the orans (early Christian prayer position), her position directly under the figure of Christ as Good Shepherd has led some to the conclusion that this is evidence for women as clergy in the early church. This is highly disputed, with some even suggesting that it is actually a male figure. The Roman catacombs were sealed in the 6th century to prevent looting, but the Catacombs of Priscilla were rediscovered in the 16th century and the majority of objects originally inside, such as sarcophagi, jewellery and liturgical objects, had been looted by the time archaeologists began investing in the 19th century. After an extensive five-year renovation, the catacombs have been recently reopened.

# Dome Mosaic of the Arian Baptistery

547 CE **Ravenna, Italy**

**FOUNDED BY** King Theodoric the Great   **STYLE** Early Byzantine
**MATERIALS** Glass and stone tesserae

The city of Ravenna on the Adriatic Sea in the north-east of Italy, was made capital of the Western Roman Empire in 402. By the end of the century, the Germanic group known as the Ostrogoths created an Italian kingdom including Ravenna that lasted from 493 until 553. During this time King Theodoric the Great launched a major building plan, including the Arian Baptistery. The Ostrogoths were Arian, a sect that believed that the Son (Jesus) was inferior to the Father (God) instead of parts of an equal Trinity. The Arians were deemed heretics by the Ecumenical First Council of Nicaea of 325, but continued to thrive in some Germanic areas for centuries. Theodoric decorated his religious buildings with traditional Roman mosaics, pictures created by placing small tesserae, or pieces of coloured stone and glass, to form an intricate picture. The scene from the Arian Baptistery's dome shows the baptism of a very young, almost feminine Christ by John the Baptist in the centre, along with a personification of the River Jordan. Surrounding them are processions of the Apostles led by St Peter and St Paul. These mosaics are given a rich feel by the use of gold leaf under glass, which makes them shimmer dramatically in changing light. After Justinian I conquered Ravenna in 540, the Byzantines continued to build churches with spectacular mosaics. However, the new mosaics were orthodox instead of Arian and were meant to establish and display Justinian's authority as both a religious and temporal ruler.

## Justinian I and Theodora

To symbolize the harmony between his civil and religious duties, Justinian I commissioned elaborate mosaics for the Basilica of San Vitale in Ravenna featuring his likeness and that of his wife, Empress Theodora. Placed in the apse, surrounding the altar, Justinian and his artisans chose the most sacred area of the church to demonstrate his authority.

'The mosaics of Ravenna constitute a critical phase in the understanding of the development of medieval art.'

ITTAI WEINRYB,
ART HISTORIAN

# Icon of Christ Pantocrator

6th century CE  **St Catherine's Monastery, Sinai, Egypt**

### Pantocrator Dome

Christ Pantocrator is not just a subject of icons but also of church mosaics and paintings. This example is from inside the dome of the Church of the Saviour on Spilled Blood, in St Petersburg, Russia, which was built at the end of the 19th century in honour of Alexander II.

'In the eyes of the faithful, the resemblance of the image to a holy prototype is, in fact, the raison d'être for icons representing single figures.'

MANOLIS CHATZIDAKIS, HISTORIAN

**COMMISSIONED BY** Emperor Justinian I   **MATERIALS** Encaustic on wood   **DIMENSIONS** 84.5 x 44 cm/33 x 17 in.

Orthodox Christian icons are 'windows into the divine' that physically represent Christ, the Virgin or any of the saints. As St Basil noted in the 4th century, 'The honour shown the image passes over to the archetype', meaning that a person venerating an icon is not honouring the physical object, but what it represents. Perhaps the most famous icon in existence is the Christ Pantocrator at St Catherine's Monastery, in Sinai, Egypt, which is also the oldest Christ Pantocrator in existence. It is encaustic – painted with coloured hot wax – which is the most common form of icon. Pantocrater means 'ruler over all' and icons of this type show a specific depiction of Christ: the upper half of his body with one hand raised in blessing and the other holding a Gospel book. The differences between the two sides of his face are said to represent his dual natures: man and God. Furthermore, this icon marks a major shift in the depictions of Christ from the clean-shaven young shepherd of the earliest years to the bearded man most people recognize today. The painter's style demonstrates influences from Roman portrait painting and Fayum mummy portraits. The mouth is assymetrical and the eyes are dissimilar in size and shape. The icon has great similarities to those of St Peter and the Virgin also at St Catherine's Monastery, which raises the possibility that all three icons came from the great workshops of Constantinople, perhaps even as a gift from the Emperor Justinian I. The Christ Pantocrator is one of the very few icons that survived the iconoclasm during the Byzantine Empire, when religious icons were declared forbidden and the majority were destroyed.

## The Mystic Mill

The column capitals inside the basilica were also carefully wrought. A famous example, the Mystic Mill, combines Old and New Testaments by showing Moses grinding grain into flour that Paul collects.

'Let all realize that this is meant to be John when he holds the attention of the people, pointing out Christ with his finger.'

INSCRIPTION BELOW JOHN THE BAPTIST TRUMEAU FIGURE AT VÉZELAY

# Trumeau at the Basilica of St Magdalene, Vézelay

*c.* 1120–50 CE **Vézelay, France**

**STYLE** Romanesque   **NARTHEX** 1.2 sq km/13 sq ft
**NAVE DIMENSIONS** 62 x 14 m/203 x 46 ft   **HEIGHT** 18 m/59 ft

Pilgrimage was one of the most important forms of medieval Christian devotion. There were also important relics and churches for pilgrims to visit along the way to more prominent shrines. The Basilica of St Magdalene at Vézelay performed both functions: it lies on one of the four major French routes to Santiago de Compostela in north-western Spain, and it also contained the relics of Mary Magdalene. One of the largest and finest Romanesque churches in Europe, it was built just before the transition to the Gothic style, although the choir was rebuilt in the Gothic style after the original was burned in 1165. One of the most dramatically decorated areas of the church is the set of doors leading from the narthex (porch) into the nave. As a person entered the nave, he or she would encounter scenes deeply carved into the areas above and beside each door. In the centre, on the trumeau (central column) that divides the two 'leaves' of the door, is the prominent figure of St John the Baptist, holding a dish or nimbus with the Paschal Lamb and a cross. His identity is certain thanks to an inscription identifying him below his feet. To his left and right are prophets, and directly above him is Christ. This symbolism allows him to prepare the way for visitors to the church, as he prepared the world for Christ. The basilica saw drastic declines in visitors after another monastery claimed the remains of Mary Magdalene in 1280 and the building narrowly avoided destruction during the French Revolution.

# Icon of Our Lady of Vladimir

*c.* 1130 CE  **Tretyakov Gallery, Moscow, Russia**

**ORIGIN** Constantinople  **MATERIALS** Tempera on panel
**DIMENSIONS** 104 x 69 cm/41 x 27 in.

## Theotokos

The Theotokos (Mary as 'Christ-Bearer') is a popular subject for icons, such as this one from the Hagia Sophia in Istanbul. Mary was given the title 'Theotokos' at the Council of Ephesus in 431 CE as her son is both God and man.

'It is admitted by all who have seen it to be one of the most outstanding religious paintings of the world.'

DAVID TALBOT RICE,
ART HISTORIAN

Our Lady of Vladimir, also known as Theotokos of Vladimir, is a symbol of Russia, but it was originally created in a Byzantine workshop, probably in Constantinople. In 1131, soon after it was painted, it was sent as a gift to Grand Duke Yury Dolgoruky of Kiev. His son, Andrey Bogolyubsky, brought it to Vladimir, where the Assumption Cathedral was built to house it. At this time, a riza – a silver and jewelled metal covering over all but the skin of the Virgin and Child – was attached to the icon to protect it. The painting survived fires and Mongol invasions and is said to have been brought to Moscow in order to resist Tamerlane's invasion in 1395. By 1520 it was housed permanently in Moscow in the Cathedral of the Dormition, where it became associated with the tsars and was used in the most celebrated ceremonies, such as coronations and elections of patriarchs. At this time a legend grew claiming that it had been painted by St Luke from living subjects. Regarded as the finest panel icon surviving from the 11th-century workshops of the Comnenian dynasty, Our Lady of Vladimir is an Eleusa icon, in which the Virgin and Child are shown cheek to cheek, a position known in the Western church as the Virgin of Tenderness. The reverse of the icon is painted with a 15th-century Hetoimasia – image of the prepared throne of Christ waiting for his second coming. Due to damage over the years, the only original parts of the icon are the hands and faces, although these show an emotional, human quality that differs from earlier icons.

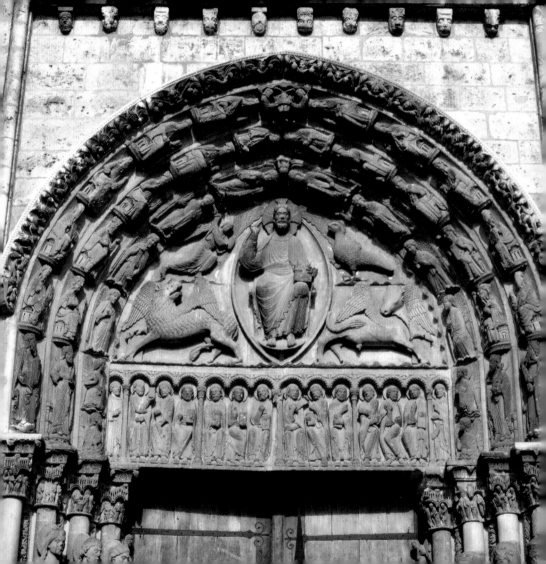

# Tympanum at Chartres Cathedral

1194–1250 CE **Chartres, France**

**MATERIAL** Stone  **DATE OF PORTAL** 1150
**HIGHEST POINT** 113 m/370 ft (16th-century spire)

One of the most important aspects of the decoration of medieval cathedrals was the portals, or doorways, through which pilgrims and worshippers entered the church. The most important images were placed above the doorway in a semicircular stone known as a tympanum. One of the most impressive of these belongs to the central doorway of the Royal Portal, part of the west facade of Chartres Cathedral. Chartres was a bishop's seat from the 4th century, but it also housed the Sancta Camisa (robe) that Mary wore at Christ's birth. Chartres was the subject of great building projects, including one in the 12th century, and then again in the 13th century when a fire destroyed most of the church. However, the western facade survived the fire, and along with it, its beautifully sculpted early Gothic portals. The middle portal is dedicated to representing Revelation 4:1-11. The tympanum itself depicts Christ in Majesty, surrounded by the four evangelical symbols (lion, ox, man and eagle). The archivolts, or bands surrounding the arch, are sculpted with the twenty-four elders of the Apocalypse. The lintel (beam) between the tympanum and the door features the Twelve Apostles in groups of three, together with the Old Testament figures of Enoch and Elijah, who prophesized the second coming of Christ. All this focuses the viewer's attention on the Christ in Majesty on the tympanum, as he sits in judgement over humankind at the end of the world. The French Gothic cathedral is a UNESCO World Heritage Site.

## Chartres Labyrinth

Set into the floor of Chartres Cathedral is a labyrinth that measures close to 12 metres (39 ft) in diameter. Built in the early 13th century, this labyrinth pavement fills the width of the nave. It is thought that the labyrinth symbolizes the long difficult journey medieval pilgrims would have made to visit pilgrimage sites such as this one. In fact, the labyrinth theme is much older than Christianity, but walking it while praying has become a modern form of devotion.

'At once I was in the Spirit, and there before me was a throne in heaven with someone sitting on it.'

REVELATION 4:2

# Madonna Enthroned

C. 1310 CE **Uffizi, Florence, Italy**

**COMMISSIONED BY** The Humiliati **ARTIST** Giotto di Bondone
**MATERIALS** Tempera on wood panel **DIMENSIONS** 325 x 204 cm/128 x 80 in.

## Cimabue's Virgin and Child Enthroned

*Virgin and Child Enthroned* (1280) by Cimabue shares many similarities with his pupil's *Madonna Enthroned*, but it is clearly more closely linked to the Italianate Byzantine style. This is evident in the more stylized drapery, the arrangement of the angels and saints and the lack of realism in light or perspective.

'Cimabue once thought that he held the field in painting, and now Giotto has the praise, so much so that the other's fame is obscured.'

DANTE, *PURGATORIO* 11

Working in 14th-century Italy, Giotto di Bondone was a student of the Florentine painter Benvenuto di Giuseppe Cimabue. Like his teacher, Giotto was influenced by the Byzantine religious painting tradition. However, his paintings are sufficiently different to later medieval art that they are considered to mark the transition to the Renaissance. Nevertheless, in many ways Giotto is firmly tied to earlier traditions. The *Madonna Enthroned* was commissioned as the altarpiece for the Franciscan Church of Ognissanti (All Saints) in Florence, which was associated with the Humiliati order, one of the mendicant orders that served the needs of the growing urban populations of Europe. Stylistically, the altarpiece bears many of the hallmarks of the early Renaissance. The angels and saints on the sides of the work are overlapped as if in real space, instead of arranged to show each face in its entirety. The throne also seems to occupy real space. Furthermore, the light is realistically portrayed with shadows and highlights instead of with heavy lines. There are still echoes of the Gothic style, recognizable in the pointed arches of Mary's throne, the Byzantine-style gold background, the much older looking face of the 'infant' Christ, and the Maestà pose of Mary in Majesty, which also originates from the Byzantine style. The most important aspect of the painting, however, may not be the newfound naturalism of the techniques used to create it, but instead the way that the style results in a dramatization of the story of Mary, reflecting a time when her cult was at the peak of its popularity. The painting is housed in the Uffizi gallery of Florence.

# Resurrection of Christ and Women at the Tomb

1440–41 CE  **Convent of San Marco, Florence, Italy**

**ARTIST** Fra Angelico   **MATERIALS** Gold leaf and tempera on wood
**DIMENSIONS** 181 x 151 cm/71¼ x 59½ in.

In 1437 the Convent of San Marco became a daughter house of the nearby Dominican house of San Dominico in Fiesole, Tuscany. Cosimo il Vecchio de' Medici, who maintained a cell at San Marco for withdrawing from the world, sponsored the renovation of the complex and commissioned Fra Giovanni of Fiesole, popularly known as Fra Angelico (the 'Angelic Friar'). Already an established fresco and panel painter, Fra Angelico painted frescoes between 1439 and 1444, including in the Chapter House, at the top of the staircase leading to the monks' cells, a madonna with saints in the church and even in the cells. One of these cell frescoes is an image of the Resurrection of Christ, an event that is described in all four Gospel accounts. By the 15th century, Italian art often showed Christ floating above his sarcophagus, as he does here. He holds a white pennant with a red cross on it, long a symbol of the Resurrection and also seen frequently in depictions of the Agnes Dei (Lamb of God). The Gospels differ in their descriptions of which women go early in the morning to anoint Jesus' body, only to discover an angel over an empty tomb. Most likely the women are Mary Magdalene, Mary mother of James and Salome, with the Virgin in blue behind them and a Dominican kneeling at the left. Fra Angelico, who had trained with Cimabue, was innovative in his artistic style. His bodies have three-dimensional weight, the drapery is realistic, the sarcophagus realistically rendered, and his use of light and shadow is masterful.

## The Annunciation

Another important fresco by Fra Angelico is located at the top of the stairs to the cells at San Marco and depicts the Annunciation. The placement of the frescoes in the monks' cells makes it clear that they were intended as superlative devotional aids.

'But it is impossible to bestow too much praise on this holy father, who was so humble and modest in all that he did and said and whose pictures were painted with such facility and piety.'

GIORGIO VASARI,
*LIVES OF THE ARTISTS* (1550)

## Adam and Eve

While the meaning of *The Garden of Earthly Delights* is mysterious, the theme of the Garden of Eden, as shown in the left panel, is an enduring one in Christian art. The first humans created by God, as told in Genesis, Adam and Eve represent innocence and its loss.

'I cannot help feeling that the real secret of his magnificent nightmares and daydreams has still to be disclosed.'

ERWIN PANOFSKY,
ART HISTORIAN

# The Garden of Earthly Delights

1480–1505 CE **Prado, Madrid, Spain**

**ARTIST** Hieronymus Bosch  **MATERIALS** Oil paint on oak
**DIMENSIONS** 220 x 195 cm/86½ x 77 in. (centre panel)

*The Garden of Earthly Delights* is one of the most mysterious works of Christian art. This Early Netherlandish work is a triptych consisting of three panels, the smaller of which close on the largest, central panel for storage or moving. This style is most associated with medieval altarpieces, but Hieronymous Bosch's work bears little resemblance to contemporary pieces from the Burgundian/Hapsburg areas of the Netherlands where he lived. Stylistically, the piece contains elements of both the Early Renaissance and the Late Gothic. The left panel shows a scene of the Garden of Eden, while the one on the right depicts a hellscape of damned souls. When the panels are folded shut, a grisaille painting of the Earth at creation is revealed. However, the interior middle panel (right) has confused viewers for centuries and left art historians divided as to whether the work is meant to mourn the loss of Paradise because of the fall of man or a moral warning to beware of the wages of sin. Whether it symbolizes lost innocence or sinful behaviour in need of punishment, the middle panel has a fantastical, dreamlike quality with its mixture of detailed nude figures, animals and enormous fruit. Art historians have noted the lack of shame in the panel, mixed with curiosity. Additionally, there are hairy figures that represent primitive humanity, another sign of innocence. The oddness of the subject matter means that its commissioning and use were likely private, although the patron is as mysterious as the piece and its painter.

# The Last Supper

*c.* 1495–98 CE  **Santa Maria delle Grazie, Milan, Italy**

**ARTIST** Leonardo da Vinci  **MATERIALS** Oil and tempera on dry plaster
**DIMENSIONS** 460 x 880 cm/173¼ x 346½ ft

### Judas Iscariot

Judas Iscariot (pictured here in green and blue) famously betrayed Jesus on the evening of the Last Supper. However, the Gospel of Judas and other early apocryphal texts praise him for his role in the events that led to the salvation of man through Christ's crucifixion.

'A picture or representation of human figures ought to be done in such a way as that the spectator may easily recognize, by means of their attitudes, the purpose in their minds.'

LEONARDO DA VINCI

Perhaps the most famous piece of religious art in the world, Leonardo da Vinci's mural of *The Last Supper* has captured the imaginations of thousands. When Ludovico Sforza, Duke of Milan, commissioned da Vinci he hoped to create a family mausoleum, as seen in the lunettes above the main supper scene with the Sforza coat of arms. His dream was not realized, however, and the work was left to grace the refectory of the convent of Santa Maria delle Grazie. The work depicts one of the seminal moments in Christ's life, as told in John 13:21, when Christ told his disciples that one of them would betray him. This was not an uncommon subject, nor was the artist's positioning of the figures on one side of the table. Da Vinci's originality is in his placement of the future traitor, Judas, on the same side, and the way in which he depicts the initial emotional reaction of each man. Da Vinci painted on dry plaster instead of wet, using new techniques that did not allow the paint to properly adhere, which caused it to flake by 1517 and continue to deteriorate badly thereafter, despite frequent attempts at restoration. Even in its current condition, it is still a powerful Renaissance masterpiece. There are also numerous clues to the work from da Vinci's own hand and workshop, the most important of which are his notebooks, twenty prefatory drawings now held in a British royal collection and a copy undertaken by his assistant, Giampietrino. From these we know that from left to right the figures are: Bartholomew, James son of Alphaeus, Andrew, Judas, Peter, John, Jesus, Thomas, James the Greater, Philip, Matthew, Jude Thaddeus and Simon.

# Praying Hands

1508 CE **Albertina Museum, Vienna, Austria**

**ARTIST** Albrecht Dürer    **MATERIALS** Ink and gouache on paper
**DIMENSIONS** 29 x 20 cm/11⅜ x 7⅞ in.

Albrecht Dürer was a German artist from Nuremberg, famed for his paintings, woodcuts and copper engravings. Dürer established his reputation early in life and is often considered both the finest practitioner of Northern Renaissance art and the first artist with an international reputation because of his clever entrepreneurial skills. His prints spread widely throughout Europe and he even employed agents to sell them. Yet, his best-known work is his study of praying hands – also known as *Study of the Hands of an Apostle* – a piece not meant as a finished work but as preparation for painting the central panel of the triptych for the Heller altar. The altar, commissioned for the Dominican church in Frankfurt, was destroyed by fire in 1729, but the sketch, one of eighteen he made for the project, survived to become one of the most iconic pieces of Christian art in the world. Originally, the sketch was much larger and also included the praying apostle's head, however, in the 16th century it was cut and divided into two separate works. The disembodied hands have taken on a life of their own within popular culture; they have assumed meanings, both religious and secular, many of which Dürer could never have imagined. The likeness of *Praying Hands* can be seen on T-shirts, posters, pendants, coffee mugs and mobile phone cases. It is also the subject of tattoos and an Andy Warhol print. Its power as an image in popular religion is supported by the numerous false stories about its creation, including the myth that the drawing depicts the hands his brother ruined while supporting Albrecht's artistic studies by working in a mine.

## The Twelve Apostles

The disciples and companions of Christ are known as the Twelve Apostles. Luke 6:12–16 tells us that after a night of prayer he chose, James, John, Philip, Bartholomew, Matthew, Thomas, James son of Alphaeus, Simon the Zealot, Jude Thaddeus, Judas Iscariot, and brothers Peter and Andrew.

'They've come to stand for a kind of religious piety, especially in the context of ordinary, working people, because the hands are rough.'

ANDREW ROBINSON, SENIOR CURATOR, NATIONAL GALLERY, WASHINGTON DC

# Sistine Chapel Ceiling

1508–12 CE **Vatican City**

**ARTIST** Michelangelo Buonarroti   **MATERIALS** Paint on plaster
**DIMENSIONS** 40.5 x 14 m / 133 x 46 ft   **CEILING HEIGHT** 21m / 681ft

## Noah

Righteous Noah was commanded to build an ark to save his family and a pair of each animal when God found the rest of the world lacking and flooded it. The Deluge is one of the most reproduced themes from the Old Testament and it also links Christianity to other traditions, such as that of ancient Mesopotamia, which has its own flood stories.

'I am not in the right place – I am not a painter.'

MICHELANGELO

When the original decoration was ruined by a long crack that opened in the ceiling of the Sistine Chapel, Pope Julius II ordered Michelangelo to accept the commission to paint the repaired ceiling. Michelangelo resented his task because he thought of himself as a sculptor and not a painter, and he felt intimidated by the scale of the commission. High above the floor on special scaffolding, Michelangelo painted central scenes that are illustrations of stories from the Book of Genesis. At the centre of the detail shown here are the three scenes telling the story of Noah, with the Flood in the middle. While the colours are bright, the subject is dark, showing a capsizing boat and figures trying futilely to escape the rising waters, with the Ark pictured in the background. It is surrounded by smaller scenes that show the drunkenness and the sacrifice of Noah. Each of these is surrounded by beautiful nude youths (usually called the Ignudi), which represent either the perfection of humanity or angels. Surrounding the main scenes are figures of sibyls and prophets, and images of biblical families. The ceiling has overseen the election of popes for 500 years. During papal conclaves, a special chimney in the room is used to signal after each vote whether or not a decision has been reached. These centuries of use required a careful restoration of the frescoes from 1980 to 1999, which revealed the original bright colours and left it in excellent condition, other than a small missing piece of plaster that fell from the Flood scene in the 18th century. More than a million tourists view the Sistine Chapel each year.

# Judith Beheading Holofernes

1598–99 CE **Palazzo Barberini, Rome, Italy**

**ARTIST** Michelangelo da Merisi Caravaggio **MATERIALS** Oil on canvas
**DIMENSIONS** 143 x 195 cm/56 ¼ x 76 ¾ in.

### Gentileschi's Judith and Holofernes

Caravaggio's work was clearly an influence on the most famous female Baroque painter, Artemisia Gentileschi, who painted at least four versions of Judith and Holofernes. This one, painted in c. 1620, is held at the Uffizi in Florence.

> 'Caravaggio's revolution was to treat biblical and mythological subjects with realism.'
>
> DAWSON CARR, CURATOR, NATIONAL GALLERY, LONDON

If Renaissance masters introduced perspective, modelling and depth to Christian paintings, then their Baroque counterparts moved from idealized figures to realistic ones. The master of this realism was Michelangelo da Merisi Caravaggio. He is almost as famous for his dramatic life, full of fights, murders and even a death warrant from the Pope, as he is for his work. This sense of drama is highly visible in his paintings, which portray the most emotionally fraught moment of each story he tells. *Judith Beheading Holofernes*, a detail of which is shown here, is typical of his style. The story is taken from the Book of Judith, one of the apocryphal Old Testament books of the Roman Catholic and Eastern Orthodox Bible that is not recognized by Judaism or Protestants. Judith was a beautiful widow who had warned the Israelites to return to their covenant with God and trust him to help them overcome their Assyrian conquerors. She seduced the Assyrian leader Holofernes, before decapitating him with his own sword to save her people. Caravaggio took this subject and concentrated on the most dramatic moment, depicting Judith just as her cut is almost complete, when Holofernes' death is assured, yet there is still a glimmer of life in his eyes. The realism is captured in the almost perfect anatomy of Holofernes and the weathered face of Judith's maid. The drama is underlined by the artist's use of tenebrism, a technique using intense chiaroscuro, featuring areas of darkness contrasted with intense areas of light from an unseen source.

# The Repentant Peter

*c.*1600 CE **San Diego Museum of Art, California, USA**

**STYLE** Mannerist   **ARTIST** El Greco   **MATERIALS** Oil on canvas
**DIMENSIONS** 93.5 x 75 cm/36 ⅞ x 29 ⅝ in.

## Mary Magdalene

Mary Magdalene (also painted here by El Greco) was a follower of Christ during his lifetime, and was present at both the Crucifixion and the Resurrection. Western Christianity conflated her with the repentant prostitute or loose woman who anointed Christ's feet, making her a symbol of both unchaste women and of repentance and forgiveness.

'It is a message to sinners that there could be forgiveness after all.'

DR JOHN MARCIARI,
CURATOR

Domenikos Theotokópoulos, better known as El Greco (the Greek), trained as an icon painter in Crete before leaving for Italy, where he studied with masters, such as Titian and Tintoretto, in Venice and Rome from 1567 to 1576. After failing to achieve artistic success in Italy, El Greco was lured to Spain by the possible patronage of Philip II, but the king was not pleased with his style. The painter eventually found recognition when he settled in Toledo, where he forged his reputation painting portraits and religious works and made his fortune. *The Repentant Peter* was one of his favourite themes, with at least six examples existing, and another six attributed to other artists in his workshop. This saintly portrait depicts St Peter's distress caused by his denial of Christ prior to his crucifixion. However, despite this weighty topic, it is a work of great hope and forgiveness, for Mary Magdalene is seen in the lower left corner, running to tell St Peter of Christ's resurrection. This scene resonated with El Greco and his contemporaries because of the emphasis on the sacrament of penance and confession by the Counter-Reformation. Artistically, many have noted the relationship between El Greco's use of bright blues, yellows and pinks and his training in Venice, an area renowned for using colours like these, but in landscapes. The artist adopts a close-up view of Peter, who is lit by an ethereal light, which gives the portrait a great intensity. Most apparent, however, is that El Greco elongated his figures in the Mannerist style of painting, which represented an imaginative pause between the more realistic Renaissance and Baroque periods in Italy.

# An Elderly Man as St Paul

*c.* 1659 CE **National Gallery, London, UK**

**ARTIST** Rembrandt van Rijn **MATERIALS** Oil paint on canvas
**DIMENSIONS** 102 x 85.5 cm/40⅛ x 33¾ in.

### St Peter Repentant

An earlier work by Rembrandt, which was painted in *c.* 1631 and is titled *St Peter Repentant*, shows a remorseful Peter in prison following his denial of Jesus. As in Rembrandt's painting of Paul, Peter is depicted alone and with his hands clasped. Rembrandt's use of light emphasizes Peter's isolation and the darkness that surrounds him.

'A work is finished when the master has achieved his intention in it.'

REMBRANDT VAN RIJN

The Protestant Reformation changed almost every aspect of Christianity, including the role of religious art. In the 17th century, the Netherlands, a republic led by a merchant middle class, exemplified many of the new Protestant trends. Dutch Protestantism emphasized a personal, internal relationship with God and preferred paintings that reflected the values of simplicity in daily life. An estimated two million paintings and prints were produced in the 17th-century Netherlands, but most of these were still lifes or depictions of virtuous, hardworking Dutch, such as milkmaids. Yet, there was still a Protestant market for religious art, a niche that Rembrandt filled with skill and beauty. His style was much influenced by Caravaggio's anatomical realism and dramatic use of light and chiaroscuro. However, Rembrandt set himself apart from Caravaggio in a number of ways. First, he did not pick the most dramatic moments for his subjects, and instead focused on contemplative ones. For example, here St Paul is not depicted in the midst of his conversion on the road to Damascus. Instead, his hands are quietly clasped as he gazes softly, eyes turned to the side. Paul's face is rendered with Rembrandt's characteristic luxurious brushwork and thick paint. This contemplative depiction of Paul was consistent with the Protestant emphasis on salvation by faith alone. This work was painted towards the end of Rembrandt's career at a time when quiet, internal prayer was still in demand, but a new vogue for idealized subjects had been introduced. Rembrandt ignored this commercial trend and painted some of his best-known religious portraits during this period.

# Rose Window, León

1849 CE **León Cathedral, Spain**

**ARTIST** P. Ibáñez **MATERIALS** Stained glass, stone tracery
**STYLE** Gothic **NAVE DIMENSIONS** 90 x 40 m/295 x 131 ft

In Romanesque architecture, the Roman oculus (opening) evolved into a round window, usually on the west side of the church. However, these windows tended to be small because of the architectural limitations of load-bearing walls. Gothic architecture used flying buttresses and ribbed vaults to relieve the stresses on outer walls, leaving architects free to design churches with much thinner walls and much larger windows. Around the year 1200 true rose windows began to be included, first in France, but soon after in England, Spain, Germany and Italy. While the earliest rose windows tended to be found above west doors and were associated with the Last Judgement, soon they were also being included on the transept ends to the north and south, where the Virgin Mary was frequently honoured. The rose window did not get its name until the 17th century, when they were no longer being produced, but they experienced a resurgence in the 19th century as a major feature of Gothic Revival architecture, by which time they had become even more closely associated with Mary because of their name and Bernard of Clairvaux's famous quote (see right). This beautiful example is from León Cathedral in north-western Spain, which was rebuilt in the 13th century in a strict French Gothic style, complete with three rose windows. The original southern window was dismantled after being damaged in the earthquake of 1755, but was redesigned by a Jesuit during a later restoration in 1849. The subject is the typical one of the Virgin Mary enthroned, holding Christ and surrounded by the Twelve Apostles in the inner 'petals'.

## Church of San Pedro

While the Gothic stained-glass rose window is of French origin, Spain's 12th-century Church of San Pedro in Ávila, only 250 km (155 miles) from León, has a large Romanesque round window that foreshadows it. This rose window with its Cistercian design is the most striking feature of the facade at San Pedro. Rose windows appeared in Spanish churches from the 11th century.

'In Mary we see a rose, soothing everybody's hurts, giving the destiny of salvation back to all.'

BERNARD OF CLAIRVAUX

# The Good Samaritan

1890 CE **Kröller-Müller Museum, Otterlo, Netherlands**

**ARTIST** Vincent van Gogh  **MATERIALS** Oil paint on canvas
**DIMENSIONS** 73 x 60 cm / 28¾ x 23⅝ in.

On 8 May 1889, Vincent van Gogh, fearing a recurrence of the breakdown that had sent him to the hospital at Arles, admitted himself to the Saint-Paul-de-Mausole asylum in Saint-Rémy, Provence. There he continued to paint, setting up a studio in another cell of the former monastery, where he was often kept indoors by the weather, and was forced to stay in the grounds when he went outside. His solution was to paint more than thirty studies from his collection of prints, including one from a black and white print of Eugène Delacroix's *The Good Samaritan* (see right), which was painted in 1852. This allowed van Gogh to continue his exploration of colour, as well as his distinctive Post-Impressionist style of painterly lines and brushstrokes. Perhaps more importantly, this study of the Good Samaritan allowed a desperate man a connection with one of the driving forces in his life: Christianity. Van Gogh was the son of a minister of the Dutch Reformed Church and had sought to become a minister himself after disappointment in love while living in England. He was denied entrance to the School of Theology in Amsterdam because he refused to learn Latin and he quickly lost a job ministering to the workers in the mining communities of the south of Belgium because he was too unorthodox in his approach. In Saint-Rémy, at the end of his life, van Gogh returned to religious themes, including the pietà and the Crucifixion. *The Good Samaritan*, a detail of which is shown here, blends religious solace with the pinnacle of Van Gogh's creativity; during the same period he also painted 120 original works, including *Irises* and *The Starry Night* (both 1889).

## Delacroix's Good Samaritan

Van Gogh and Delacroix both chose as their subject the Good Samaritan, from the parable told in Luke 10:25-37. The story tells of a man who was robbed and beaten, then ignored by both a priest and a Levite, before being generously helped by a travelling Samaritan, who becomes a lesson in kindness taught by Christ.

'I am not indifferent, and pious thoughts often console me in my suffering.'

VINCENT VAN GOGH

### The Blind Man's Meal

Another painting with spiritual resonance from Picasso's Blue Period is *The Blind Man's Meal*. This striking work was painted in Barcelona in the autumn of 1903. Like many of the Blue Period works, it depicts a solitary figure against an empty background and the blue palette conveys a mood of melancholy. The figure has been compared to Christ and the jug of wine and bread are said to represent the poor and infirm sharing in the Eucharist and through it God's grace.

'The purpose of art is washing the dust of daily life off our souls.'

PABLO PICASSO

# Mother and Child

*c.* 1901 CE **Harvard Art Museum, Cambridge, USA**

**ARTIST** Pablo Picasso **MATERIALS** Oil paint on canvas
**DIMENSIONS** 97.5 x 112 cm/38⅜ x 44 in.

In 1901, twenty-year-old Pablo Picasso began visiting Paris with his friend Carlos Casagemas. When Casagemas committed suicide the same year, Picasso entered into a deep depression and began his Blue Period, which lasted from 1901 to 1904. Picasso had been influenced by the Symbolists, especially Paul Gauguin, Henri de Toulouse-Lautrec and Edvard Munch, a fact that the work of his Blue Period makes clear. The Symbolists had started as a French literary movement that believed art should express emotion or ideas that could not be shown through naturalism, and for them the colour blue was associated with intense sadness or despair. Picasso's Blue Period subjects were the poor, beggars, prostitutes and other outsiders who are similar to the kind of figures to whom Christ ministered in the New Testament. The subject of mother and child was of intense interest to Picasso, both in the Blue Period and again later in the 1920s. In the Blue Period *Mother and Child* canvases, the figures could be the Madonna and Child and, at the same time, a contemporary homeless mother and child. The atheist Picasso was interested in mysticism and was drawn to the religious feeling in El Greco's work, imitating the Greek artist's elongated figures and cold tonality, as can be seen in the detail shown here. Perhaps more important is the feeling that his Blue Period works share with El Greco's, one that allows the spiritual lives of his subjects to shine and rise above everyday reality. At the time, these sombre works were not popular with galleries or patrons and the Blue Period was a time of poverty for Picasso. Today, however, they are among his most popular works.

# Stained Glass, Axial Chapel

1968–74 CE **Reims Cathedral, France**

**COMMISSIONED BY** Committee of Builders of Champagne-Ardenne
**ARTIST** Marc Chagall **HEIGHT** 10 m/33 ft **AREA** 75 sq m/807 sq ft

Marc Chagall, a Belarussian-born French Jewish artist, was part of the heyday of modernism before World War I in Paris. Chagall was not only a painter, he also worked in a wide range of media, including illustration, opera sets, ceramics, tapestries and prints. In 1957 he also started to design stained glass with the Jacques Simon Workshop in the city of Reims, including pieces for Metz Cathedral, the United Nations and the Rockefeller Chapel in Pocantico Hills. When a committee decided to replace the 19th-century windows in the medieval cathedral of Reims, it commissioned Chagall to make them. The cathedral still had one of its medieval windows in the apse, near the axial chapel, and the artist spent time contemplating this window, taking care to reproduce the colours in his work. He designed a triptych, each section consisting of two tall lancet windows topped with a small round window. The central window is devoted to the major figures of the Old and New Testaments: Abraham and Christ. The lower portion features scenes from Abraham's life, while the upper scenes show the Passion of Christ. The round window is a depiction of the Trinity. The left window is dedicated to the genealogy of Mary, to whom the cathedral is dedicated. The lower portion of the right window is reserved for the important moments of the lives of the kings of France who were crowned at Reims, including the baptism of Clovis, the first king of the Franks, and the coronation of St Louis, France's only canonized king. The upper portion includes New Testament parables and a round window depicting the Last Judgement.

## Modern Forms

While Marc Chagall was careful to reproduce medieval colours in his stained glass, his figures are decisively modern in their simplicity and broken-up forms.

'...it is a creative force which appears and bears me, while the lead cuts and the colour emerges. It is this interior life that the painter with magic mysteriously encloses in his work.'

MARC CHAGALL

# Tombs, Memorials, Death and Resurrection

# Catacombs of San Callisto

2nd century CE  **Rome, Italy**

**COMMISSIONED BY** Pope Zephyrinus  **ARCHITECT** Not known
**DEPTH** 20 m/66 ft  **AREA** 36 hectares/90 ac.

### St Cecilia

Cecilia (seen here in a painting by Guido Reni) was a 3rd-century martyr from a noble Roman family and the patron saint of musicians and church music. She is one of the many saints who were originally buried at San Callisto. A statue to Cecilia still stands in her crypt in the catacombs, although her remains were removed to the Basilica of St Cecilia in Trastevere in 821.

'There is a natural awe and reverence for these ancient burial places.'

JOHN HENRY PARKER, *THE CATACOMBS OF ROME* (1877)

Prior to the legalization of Christianity in 313 CE, growing numbers of Christians created a need for large areas to be used for inhumation burial. The catacombs, reaching to more than 20 metres (66 ft) below the ground, offered privacy and enough space. The catacombs were extended gradually, with most Christians being wrapped in linen and placed in loculi – burial niches sealed with a slab. A few wealthier families could afford to build cubicula, or small rooms with multiple loculi, which were often decorated with some of the earliest examples of Christian scenes and symbols. The catacombs were also important in the development of the cult of the saints and early Christians visited them on the anniversary of a martyr's death. The Catacombs of San Callisto hold the tombs of many martyrs and sixteen popes. They are named after the deacon Callixtus, who administered them at the request of Pope Zephyrinus in the first decades of the 3rd century. Contrary to popular belief, the catacombs were not commonly used as hiding places during periods of persecution; instead they probably served as a safe place to celebrate the sacrament of the Eucharist during difficult periods. The catacombs continued to be used after legalization for burials and veneration of martyrs until Rome began to be sacked, starting with the first raid in 410. By the end of the 9th century, the relics of saints had been moved to churches above ground for safety and the catacombs were sealed and largely forgotten until their rediscovery in the 17th century. The Catacombs of San Callisto are among the largest in Rome and contain *c.* 500,000 tombs.

# Christian Sarcophagus

C. 312 CE **Metropolitan Museum, New York, USA**

**ORIGIN** Rome   **MATERIAL** Carrara marble
**DIMENSIONS** 66 x 213 x 58 cm/26 x 84 x 23 in.

In 313 Constantine the Great, the first Christian Roman Emperor, released the Edict of Milan, making Christianity legal and tolerated throughout the Roman Empire. This acceptance allowed Christians to more openly portray their faith, including Romans who Christianized Roman burial practices. During the Republic, Romans had cremated their dead, placing the ashes in urns and ossuaries. However, in the first centuries of the empire, the Romans shifted towards the inhumation practice of the Greeks and Etruscans. By the first half of the 2nd century, Rome had become a great centre of sarcophagi production in order to accommodate this shift. The sarcophagi were worked mostly in marble from Carrara in northern Italy, but also in other stone and wood. The most popular subjects for the carvings were Greek mythology, garlands and biographical scenes from the lives of the dead. Roman Christians preferred inhumation and adapted the practice to suit their own beliefs. This example shows how scenes from the lives of Christ and St Peter could be substituted for personal events or myths. Here Christ's entry into Jerusalem at the beginning of the Passion narrative is shown, which is of great importance to all Christians. Other scenes include the miraculous feeding of the multitudes and the raising of Lazarus. Originally the miraculous cure of the blind man was also featured, but when the sarcophagus was restored in 1910 the blind man's feet – all that remained – were mistakenly used for the likeness of a frightened child in the entry into Jerusalem scene. The scenes from St Peter's life, including his arrest seen here, are those that link him to Rome.

## Sarcophagi Mythology

Non-Christian Roman sarcophagi (literally 'flesh-eating' in Greek) were frequently covered with scenes from mythology. This 3rd-century sarcophagus, which is housed in the National Roman Museum at Palazzo Altemps, shows the twelve labours of Hercules, the Greek hero.

'They, then, who are destined to die, need not be careful to inquire what death they are to die, but into what place death will usher them.'

ST AUGUSTINE OF HIPPO, *CITY OF GOD* (5TH CENTURY)

## St Cuthbert's Pectoral Cross

The most famous example of an Anglo-Saxon pectoral cross is St Cuthbert's, which is also made of gold and garnets. It was found hung around his neck on a silk and gold cord and buried deeply in his garments, which perhaps explains how it survived Henry VIII's purge of the monasteries.

'So they washed the virgin's body, and having clothed it in new garments, brought it into the church, and laid it in the sarcophagus.'

BEDE, DESCRIBING THE BURIAL OF ST AETHELTHRYTH

# Anglo-Saxon Gold Burial Cross

*c.* 650–80 CE **Cambridge, England, UK**

**ORIGIN** England  **MATERIALS** Gold, garnet
**DIAMETER** 3.5 cm/1⅜ in.

For a century after the mission of St Augustine of Canterbury in 597, the Anglo-Saxon kingdoms saw a slow process of conversion. It was often top-down, meaning that royalty and nobility converted first, followed afterwards by the lower classes. The discovery in 2011 of the burial of a young girl of around sixteen years supports this model of conversion in Cambridgeshire. Her grave in Trumpington is unusual because it is a 'bed burial', or a burial in which she was literally laid to rest on a bed complete with wooden frame, metal brackets and lacing. It is also noteworthy because she was buried with a gold pectoral cross, which is meant to be worn on the chest. This cross signifies the girl as Christian, but also one of high status because of the value of the gold and the garnets with which it was inlaid, which would have been imported from the Black Sea or Asia. The cross was not simply grave goods, but something that she also wore in life. This can be seen from the wear on the loops on the back, which were used to sew the cross to her clothing. The other four examples of pectoral crosses also found during the same archaeological excavation in England are all meant to be pendants hung from a cord or a chain. The grave discovery of 2011 and the ornate cross have given rise to the possibility that the girl was a royal nun or abbess and that Trumpington was home to a hitherto unknown monastery or convent, perhaps like the ones founded by the royal St Aethelthryth in the 7th century.

# Reliquary of
# the True Cross

9th century CE **Metropolitan Museum, New York, USA**

**ORIGIN** Constantinople   **MATERIALS** Cloisonné enamel, silver gilt, silver, gold, niello   **DIMENSIONS** 3 x 10 x 7 cm/1 x 4 x 2¾ in.

### St Helena

Helena of Constantinople was Emperor Constantine's mother and a devout Christian. She is credited with travelling to the province of Syria Palaestina and discovering the True Cross.

'She worshipped not the wood, but the King, Him who hung on the wood. She burned with an earnest desire of touching the guarantee of immortality.'

ST AMBROSE ON ST HELENA

Soon after Christianity became legal, many Romans began to search for relics, the physical remains of saints or objects associated with Christ. One of the most holy of these is the True Cross, upon which Christ was crucified. Portions of the True Cross and other relics were protected in special containers known as reliquaries. Due to their holy contents, reliquaries tended to be made of the most costly materials by the most superior craftsmen. The reliquary shown here was made for a piece of the True Cross around the year 800, probably in the Byzantine capital of Constantinople, which was then home to the best workshops. It is in the shape of a box with a sliding lid and five interior compartments. The lid features the delicate cloisonné work for which the Byzantines were renowned, which uses very delicate wire to separate the compartments that were then filled with brightly coloured enamels. The lid's theme reflects the reliquary's contents, showing the living Christ on the cross, with a mourning Mary on one side and St John on the other. Surrounding the main scene are the busts of fourteen saints. The underside of the lid is engraved with four scenes from Christ's life: the Annunciation, Nativity, Crucifixion and Descent into Hell. The etched lines of the scenes are filled with niello, a black mixture of metals that gives depth to the scenes. This was a technique mastered by the Kievan Rus, who had contact with Byzantium for trade and its use here may demonstrate early Byzantine contact with Scandinavians.

# Birka Silver Cross

mid 10th century CE   **Swedish History Museum, Stockholm, Sweden**

**ORIGIN** Birka, Björkö, Sweden   **MATERIAL** Silver
**DIMENSIONS** 16 x 16 mm/⅝ x ⅝ in.

Scandinavia was one of the last areas of Europe to be converted
to Christianity. This push for conversion began with St Anskar,
known as the 'Apostle of the North'. After a request from the
Swedish king Björn for a Christian priest, Louis the Pious sent
Anskar and an assistant, a friar named Witmar, north. At the
Swedish town of Birka, on the island of Björkö in Lake Mälaren,
Anskar preached and evangelized for six months. Before departing
they left their new congregation in the hands of the king's
steward, Hergeir, to whom they gave the title praefectus. Birka
was one of the earliest cities established in Sweden, with close
to 1,000 inhabitants when it was at its largest. It was a trade
hub linking Scandinavia to the Baltic and the Kievan Rus, and,
ultimately, to the Byzantines and the Abbasid caliphate based in
Baghdad. Birka flourished from c. 750 to 975 and today, although
only archaeological remains survive, they offer important clues
as to how successful the early conversions to Christianity were
in Scandinavia. All written sources of the period are from the
perspective of the Christian missionaries because the Scandinavian
rune system was not used or intended for long written works.
However, out of 1,100 excavated graves at Birka, ten female graves
contained silver cross-shaped pendants (although one of these
was a male-female double burial). This suggests that Christianity's
message may have been particularly appealing to women. In most
of these graves, the women's jewellery were the only grave goods,
which underlines their importance. The simple production of the
pendants points to a symbolic value rather than a material one.

## Thor's Hammer

The double grave at Birka also
held a pendant of Thor's hammer,
a symbol of the native pagan
religion, found in more than
thirty male graves. This shows
that although conversion was
occurring, it was not society-wide
in the 10th century.

'There were many who
were well disposed
towards their mission and
who willingly listened to
the teaching of the Lord.'

RIMBERT,
*LIFE OF ANSKAR* (C.865)

## Effigy of Richard I Coeur de Lion

*c.* 1200 CE **Rouen Cathedral, France**

**STYLE** Norman  **MATERIALS** Limestone, paint, gilt
**LENGTH** 1.9 m/6¼ ft

### Richard's Heart

When Richard the Lionheart died in 1199, his heart was embalmed and buried separately. The small lead box in which Richard's heart was discovered in 1838 also bears an inscription that identifies the contents as the heart of Richard I of England. In 2013 forensic experts analysed the heart; they could not determine the cause of death, but they ruled out a theory that he was killed by a poisoned arrow.

'My corpse will be buried in Fontevraud, my heart in my cathedral of Rouen, and my entrails will stay in Chalus.'

RICHARD I TO HIS MOTHER, ELEANOR OF AQUITAINE

In the 12th century, funerary monuments in churches adopted the old Etruscan form of recumbent effigies, or likenesses. Most often carved in relief in stone, these likenesses gained popularity and became more elaborate during the later Middle Ages. One of the earlier examples is the effigy of Richard I Coeur de Lion in Rouen Cathedral. It is not Richard's only effigy because his body was divided up after his death as was the custom. At his own request, the king's entrails were buried where he died in Chalus while his body joined his father's in Fontevraud Abbey in Anjou and he sent his heart to Rouen Cathdral, to join his Norman predecessors. The division of the bodies of kings took place because it spread the honour of being a king's burial place and because it allowed for the embalming of the organs, an important factor when a sign of holiness was the lack of bodily decay after death. A recent analysis of Richard's heart, buried within a lead-lined box, revealed that it was treated with myrtle, daisy, mint, creosote, mercury and substantial quantities of frankincense before being wrapped in linen. Frankincense has special religious meaning because of its association with Christ. The effigy was at some point buried less than a metre (3 ft) under the floor of the choir and was only rediscovered after excavation in 1838, along with his heart, still in its box, in a wall nearby. The inscription on the effigy clearly states that it marks the burial of the heart of Richard, King of the English, called the Lionheart.

## Damnation

Although medieval texts tend to emphasize the salvation offered by Christ at the Last Judgement, artistic depictions tended to focus on the consequences of a refusal, such as these souls being carried to Hell at the Last Judgement. Damnation and the horrors of hell provided a more dramatic theme for artists.

'One becomes, sometimes, a little incoherent in talking about it; one is ashamed to be as extravagant as one wants to be.'

SIR ISAAC NEWTON ON THE BOOK OF REVELATION

# The Last Judgement

13th century CE  **Chartres Cathedral, France**

**STYLE** High Gothic    **MATERIALS** Stained glass, stone
**DIAMETER OF WINDOW** 12 m/39 ft

Chartres Cathedral is one of the most celebrated medieval churches because of the exceptional condition of its Gothic architecture. It was rebuilt in the Gothic style after a fire in 1194 destroyed all but the east end and the Sancta Camisa — the tunic believed to have been worn by Mary when she gave birth to Jesus. This rebuilding includes some of the most renowned stained glass in the world, with what many believe are the finest colours ever achieved in glass. The nave was completed first, making the western facade the oldest rebuilt structure, including a beautiful example of a rose window featuring the Last Judgement. The maturing Gothic style included the ability of artisans to tell a much more cohesive story in their work and the story that the western facade at Chartres tells is that of the Book of Revelation and Christ's Last Judgement of human souls. Christ is in the centre, surrounded by angels and the symbols of the Evangelists. The middle ring features the Apostles, more angels, the damned, the saved and St Michael. The outer ring depicts more angels, souls rising, saved souls, souls headed to Hell, and the Mouth of Hell. These layers are arranged in a 'wheel' with stone tracery in the shape of columns forming the spokes, radiating from the centre to capitals supporting arches that in turn support the outer medallions. These stone elements fall away when the window is viewed from the inside, leaving the masterful geometry of the designer clearly displayed. The windows were carefully dismantled, stored and then reinstalled in order to protect them during the two world wars, and much of the original stained glass in the window remains.

## The Gero Crucifix

The Gero Crucifix (c. 970) is believed to be the earliest large crucifix from north of the Alps. It was commissioned by Gero, Archbishop of Cologne, and has always been housed at Cologne Cathedral. Made of painted and gilded oak wood, the life-size figure portends the coming power and popularity of the crucifix in the high Middle Ages.

'Do not fear anything and look again at the crucifix.'

AGNES BLANNBEKIN, SAINT AND CHRISTIAN MYSTIC

# Corpus of Christ

*c.* 1250 CE **possibly Paris, France**

**MATERIALS** Elephant ivory, paint
**DIMENSIONS** 16.7 x 4.3 x 3.4 cm/6⅝ x 1¾ x 1½ in.

The Corpus of Christ – an ivory sculpture of the Crucifixion intended to hang from a cross on a church altar – demonstrates both the changing economic realities and the popular religious piety of the 13th century. Ivory had been a luxury good throughout most of the Middle Ages. Imported mainly from Africa and denoting purity and chastity, it was utilized in religious artefacts, especially in book covers and reliquaries. After a brief pause in trade, ivory became a more abundant but still expensive commodity around 1250, giving rise to new uses, including religious pieces and personal items, such as combs. The practice of using a crucifix instead of a plain cross started in the early Middle Ages, but by 1250 it had become a central part of Western spirituality and a feature of Gothic art. Monks, nuns, priests and laypeople alike would often spend hours quietly contemplating Christ's Passion and sufferings before a crucifix. The image became so widespread that there was even a Parisian guild purely for ivory crucifix sculptors, although they also worked in other media, including stone and wood. The popularity of the crucifix is often associated with a growing desire to focus on the humanity of Christ, making him more approachable than depictions such as Christ in Majesty. The Corpus of Christ, or Body of Christ, with its sweetly sad face and downcast eyes, shows a very realistic Christ, despite the loss over time of his arms and a leg. The carving powerfully conveys Christ's corporeality and suffering. In the 14th century the trade in ivory slowed and ivory once more became rarer in religious and other uses.

# Illumination of the Martyrdom of St Polycarp

1322–40 CE **Bodleian Library, Oxford, England, UK**

**ORIGIN** Thessaloniki, Greece  **STYLE** Late Byzantine  **LANGUAGE** Greek
**MATERIAL** Parchment  **FOLIO** 28 recto  **PAGE HEIGHT** 13 cm/5¼ in.

St Polycarp represents a union of several of the most important themes of the earliest centuries of Christianity: martyrdom, apostolic succession and the veneration of saints. Polycarp was a bishop of Smyrna in the early 2nd century. More importantly, he was a disciple of the Apostle John, meaning that he represented the apostolic succession. In early Christianity the only real authority came from the Apostles, whom Christ had given the mandate to go out, preach and perform the sacrament of Eucharist. The Apostles transferred this authority to their disciples, such as Polycarp. Polycarp was martyred in the mid 150s or 160s for not burning incense to the Roman emperor. This was the most common test when someone was accused of being a Christian. Refusing to perform this patriotic duty made it publically known that the individual was a Christian, leaving even sympathetic authorities little choice but to administer punishment. Polycarp met a painful fate, being first burned and, when he was miraculously unharmed by fire, was stabbed to death. His veneration exemplifies how martyrs were the models of virtuous Christian behaviour. Even after Christianity became legal, martyrs continued to be some of the most admired saints. Polycarp is seen here in a Byzantine manuscript illumination from a codex painted for the consolation of the soul of a man named Demetrios. It contains an illustration of a saint for every day of the year, giving its reader a formative figure in the church on which to meditate.

## The Golden Legend

St Polycarp's story is familiar to Roman Catholics because of *The Golden Legend*, a very popular collection of hagiographies, or saints' lives, collected by Jacobus de Voragine around 1260.

'At the root of every miracle of healing at a martyr's shrine of late antiquity, there lay a miracle of pain.'

PETER BROWN, *THE CULT OF THE SAINTS* (1981)

# Dance of Death

1474 CE **Church of St Mary of the Rocks, Beram, Croatia**

**COMMISSIONED BY** Beram Confraternity of St Mary
**ARTIST** Vincent de Kastav   **MATERIALS** Paint on plaster

## Holbein's Dance

German artist Hans Holbein the Younger designed a set of forty-one woodcuts of the Dance of Death for a book of religious reformist satire in 1526. It was so popular that there were eleven editions before 1562 and almost 100 imitations by the end of the century.

'Sceptre and crown are worthless here/I've taken you by the hand/For you must come to my dance.'

FROM A GERMAN DANCE OF DEATH TEXT (C. 1460)

The Dance of Death is a late medieval allegory for the inevitability of death for all people. The allegory became an important artistic theme in the 15th century, after the first – and now lost – recorded example was painted at the Saints-Innocents Cemetery in Paris. Most Dance of Death frescoes were accompanied by narrating texts and even a painted figure symbolizing the narrator. However, the example at Beram has neither. Painted in the tiny, remote Church of St Mary of the Rocks, Vincent de Kastav's version features all ten of the usual characters, but instead of being ranked by their social status as in other versions, Beram's procession shows pope, cardinal, bishop, king, queen, innkeeper, child, maimed, knight and merchant who stands by a table covered with goods. Despite the fact that these are out of order, the figures still make the point that death is unavoidable and does not care who you are or what riches you have, despite the merchant trying to pay him off. Beram's fresco also shares the key element of the allegory, which is the presence of skeletons representing death coming for each person. Again, this version is slightly different from most, with the skeletons wearing no shrouds and having oddly extended thigh bones instead of pelvises. Although not visible in painted form for a century afterwards, an interest in the allegory of the Dance of Death stems from the deep melancholy and fear caused by the Black Death in the 14th century. The allegory fell out of favour in the modern era, and when the church was renovated during the 18th century, the frescoes were painted over. They were rediscovered and conserved in 1913.

# Pietà

1498–99 CE  **St Peter's Basilica, Vatican City**

**COMMISSIONED BY** Cardinal Jean de Billheres  **MATERIAL** Carrara marble
**ARTIST** Michelangelo Buonarroti  **DIMENSIONS** 174 x 195 cm/68½ x 76¾ in.

### Early Sculpted Pietàs

The earliest sculpted pietàs are found in Germany and date to around the start of the 14th century. They are notable in their unsparing depiction of Christ's suffering, including his bleeding wounds and thin, broken body. Painted pietàs were known in Florence by Michelangelo's time, but his sculpted version was virtually without precedent.

'It is well with me only when I have a chisel in my hand.'

MICHELANGELO

Michelangelo Buonarroti is one of the world's best-known artists, often remembered for his magnificent paintings on the ceiling of the Sistine Chapel in the Apostolic Palace, the Pope's residence in the Vatican City. Yet, his preferred medium was marble, and he was most fulfilled when sculpting. The pietà – an image of the Virgin Mary holding her lifeless son Jesus – was one of the artist's favourite subjects, and the sculpture in the Vatican is one of his most purely Renaissance pieces with its lifelike proportions, figures and drapery folds. This pietà was commissioned by French Cardinal Jean de Billheres as a funerary monument for his tomb at the Chapel of Santa Petronilla, also in Rome. It was later moved to St Peter's when Donato Bramante was rebuilding the basilica and the original chapel had to be torn down. Michelangelo's interpretation of the pietà was different to others in that it portrayed a youthful Mary rather than an older woman. It is the only work that Michelangelo ever signed, and he did it only because he heard that it was being attributed to Cristoforo Solari. Later he felt ashamed of his self-regarding action in carving his name on the sash worn by the Virgin and swore never to sign another work again. Aside from being important within Michelangelo's body of work, his pietà is telling in what it depicts – the most emotionally wrenching event of the Virgin Mary's life. Roman Catholics of the late medieval and early modern period searched for moments of strong emotion in the lives of Christ and his mother, and Catholic art often focused on the approachable and universally understood emotion of a mother's love for her son.

# Crucifixion

1954 CE  **Metropolitan Museum, New York, USA**

**ORIGINAL NAME** *Corpus Hypercubus*   **ARTIST** Salvador Dalí
**MATERIALS** Oil paint on canvas   **DIMENSIONS** 194 x 124 cm/76½ x 48¾ in.

In 1951, Salvador Dalí – renowned as one of the greatest Surrealist artists – wrote an essay entitled 'Mystical Manifesto' in which he stated that the advent of the nuclear age, specifically the dropping of an atomic bomb on Hiroshima on 6 August 1945, 'sent a seismic shock' through him. Afterwards he wanted to 'penetrate to the core of reality' through mysticism, reaching out for personal experience of God more in the manner of St Theresa of Avila than in the way of modern academic artists. Returning to the Catholic roots of his mother, combined with the science and mathematics of his atheist father, Dalí started painting religious scenes, but ones that had his own modern twist. Architect Juan de Herrera's 16th-century Treatise on Cubic Form also influenced him. This *Crucifixion* – renamed when it was obtained by the Metropolitan Museum in New York a year later – is one of the foremost examples of Dalí's religious turn and change of artistic style in the 1950s. His choice of the Crucifixion as subject is traditional in the sense that it was meant to be an object of contemplation, just as it would have been during the Middle Ages. However, his 'nuclear mysticism' demonstrates both the influence of Italian Renaissance masters and modern science with his depiction of the cross. Instead of the usual wooden cross, Dalí uses a hypercube or four-dimensional cube. The cube's eight cells are visible in the eight cubes that make up the cross. However, unlike medieval crucifixions, Dalí obscures the face of Christ by turning it away from the viewer, but includes the personal touch of his wife Gala as Mary Magdalene in the lower left of the canvas.

## The Madonna of Port Lligat

Not all of Dalí's mystical, religious work deals with such dark subject matter as *Crucifixion*. Modelled on his wife Gala, the painting *The Madonna of Port Lligat* (1949) returns to the mother and child theme in a style that is reminiscent of the architectural throned versions of the Renaissance.

'Dali's later art explores the subjects of quantum physics and genetics with a metaphysical vision.'

IONA MILLER,
SCIENCE ARTIST

# Martyrs

2014 CE  St Paul's Cathedral, London, England, UK

**ARTISTS** Bill Viola and Kira Perov   **MEDIUM** Colour film on four vertical plasma screens   **METAL STAND DESIGNER** Norman Foster

Video installation is a contemporary art form that emerged out of video art in the 1970s. One of the pioneers of this medium is Bill Viola, an internationally acclaimed installation artist from New York, whose work has frequently focused on spiritual themes. Viola and his wife and artistic partner, Kira Perov, were commissioned to design the video installation *Martyrs* for St Paul's Cathedral in London. Norman Foster designed the cast iron supports for the plasma screens. Subtitled 'Earth, Air, Fire, Water', the installation runs on a loop, apart from short breaks during church services. The video shows four individuals experiencing a short-lived moment of respite before being pummelled by one of the four classical elements. Each individual maintains their resolve as the elements assault them. The video runs for seven minutes and has no sound. The word 'martyrs' has a particular meaning for Viola, who sees a parallel between its original meaning of 'witness' (from the Greek word) and the way in which mass media forces all people into being passive witnesses of suffering. In a continuation of this theme, Viola's depictions of nameless martyrs are placed at the end of the Dean's Aisle, in the furthest east end of the church – an area that once contained an altar dedicated to martyrs. Although the *Martyrs* installation at St Paul's has been generally well received, it has not been immune to criticism. It is the first moving-image artwork to be installed in a British cathedral or church on a long-term basis. The permanent installation belongs to the Tate but is on long-term loan to St Paul's. A second companion installation, *Mary*, is planned for 2015.

## The Four Holy Gospels

Japanese contemporary artist Makoto Fujimura illuminated *The Four Holy Gospels* in 2011 to commemorate the 400th anniversary of the King James Bible. It was the first time an artist had been commissioned to illuminate the Gospels in nearly 500 years.

'There is an increased acceptance that contemporary artists have a unique contribution to make in reinvigorating and re-enchanting our churches and cathedrals.'

PAUL BAYLEY, CURATOR

Holy Words

# Codex Argenteus

6th century CE  Carolina Rediviva, Uppsala University Library, Sweden

**ORIGIN** Ravenna, Italy  **ARTIST** Not known  **FOLIOS** 188
**MATERIALS** Silver and gold ink on purple parchment

### Nicene Creed

The Council of Nicaea was the first ecumenical, or universal, meeting of church authorities and resulted in the Nicene Creed, the most common Christian profession of faith. This icon shows Emperor Constantine I and the bishops holding the creed, which was confirmed at the second ecumenical council in 381.

'The triumphal advance of Christianity among the Goths and other Germanic tribes could not be checked.'

BARBARA ALAND,
THEOLOGIAN

When Christianity became legal in 313, Constantine I sought to define the meaning of orthodox Christian belief. The first Ecumenical Council of Nicaea in 325 had to sift through a number of different Christianities with varying theological stances. One doctrine that was declared heresy was Arianism, which stated that Jesus was not eternal, and as the Son, was inferior to God the Father. However, Arian Christianity did not quickly die and it continued to grow because Arian missionaries were the first to reach and convert many of the Germanic peoples. The most famous of these missionaries was Ulfilas. Born just as Christianity became legal, Ulfilas was probably the son of captured Christians and was raised among the Goths, a Germanic people. After being made bishop of the Christian Goths, he completed a translation of the Bible from Greek into the Gothic language. As this early form of German was not a written language, Ulfilas had to create a Gothic alphabet in order to complete his work. By the 6th century, the Arian Ostrogoths, or East Goths, ruled much of Italy and it is believed that this luxury gospel, which used Ulfilas' translation, was created for an Ostrogothic king. After the Ostrogoths fell in the late 6th century, the book disappeared from history for 1,000 years, but it reappeared in Speyer, Germany in the 16th century and then in Sweden in the following century. Now known as the Codex Argenteus, or Silver Codex, only 188 folios of the original 336 still exist, yet this manuscript is of unparalleled importance for linguists and scholars of the New Testament. Part of the Codex is on display at the Carolina Rediviva library in Sweden.

## Eusebius of Caesarea

Eusebius was a prolific writer and the Bishop of Caesarea, a city on the Mediterranean coast of Israel. His successor as bishop, Acacius, wrote a biography of Eusebius, but it is now lost, leaving us with only a few of Eusebius' writings on the Gospels.

'By going to the other gospels' reference numbers that are in the same row as the reference number in the table you are at and looking them up in the related passages of each gospel, you will find similar things mentioned.'

EUSEBIUS OF CAESAREA, *EPISTULA AD CARPIANUM*

# Rabbula Gospels

586 CE **Biblioteca Medicea Laurenziana, Florence, Italy**

**ORIGIN** Byzantium   **ARTIST** Rabbula   **LANGUAGE** Syriac
**SIZE** 33.5 x 26.5 cm/13¼ x 10⅜ in.   **MATERIALS** Ink on parchment

The four Gospels are parallel accounts of the life, death and resurrection of Jesus, but they do not include identical events. In order to better understand them, early Christian authorities sought aids to help them in their studies and in the 3rd century Ammonius the Alexandrian broke up the Gospels into pericopes – sets of verses that communicate a cohesive story or thought. However, when they were grouped out of order, they were impossible to read coherently. In the early 4th century, Eusebius of Caesarea remedied this problem by creating canon tables – ten pages of lists that showed where the concordances were between the Gospels. The canon tables could be placed at the front of a set of Gospels for study, but the Gospels themselves could still be read in order. These tables were found so useful that they became commonplace in both Byzantium and the West during the Middle Ages. The Rabbula Gospels are a 6th-century illuminated manuscript from the Monastery of St John of Zagba in what is now Syria. They are written in Syriac, which is read from right to left. The page shown here, folio 6v, features one of the tables of pericopes that appear in all four Gospels, with a column for each book. Using dividing architectural columns with arches above was very common throughout the Middle Ages, even in books that had little other decoration. The Rabbula tables also provide valuable information about early Christian art and iconography. Folio 6v shows the canon tables and features miniatures in the margins depicting Zephaniah and Nahum, two minor prophets, as well as the Healing of the Son of the Widow of Nain.

# The Book of Kells

*c. 800 CE*  **Trinity College Library, Dublin, Ireland**

**LANGUAGE** Latin  **PRIMARY SCRIPT** Insular majuscule  **MATERIAL** Vellum
**FOLIOS** 340 bound into four volumes  **DIMENSIONS** 33 x 25 cm/13 x 9 ¾ in.

### Illuminated Manuscripts

Illustrated manuscripts helped to preserve Christian literature during the barbarian invasions of Europe in the Middle Ages. Created in the late 7th or early 8th century, Northumbria's Lindisfarne Gospels combine Anglo-Saxon and Celtic traditions with those of Rome and the East.

'I've lived through many ages. I've seen suffering in the darkness. Yet I have seen beauty thrive in the most fragile of places. I have seen the book. The book that turned darkness into light.'

AISLING, FROM *THE SECRET OF KELLS* (2009)

Around the year 800, Columban monks, based either on the Scottish island of Iona or at Kells in County Meath, Ireland, created the Book of Kells, a set of the four Gospel books of the New Testament on valuable vellum, each page painstakingly hand-lettered and illustrated. In this unique artwork of the Columban monastic world, the monks used jewel-toned pigments that were brighter and more varied than other books of the time, and applied none of the gold or silver gilt so prevalent in other luxurious illuminated manuscripts. The Book of Kells, which is also known as the Book of Columba, is remarkable for the dominance of the square and cross, two of the most holy geometrical structures. It abounds with full-page illustrations, including the first portrait of the Virgin Mary in a Western manuscript, portraits of the four evangelists who wrote the gospels (Matthew, Mark, Luke and John) and four richly decorated pages that take as their subject the opening word or words of the four gospels. Shown opposite is a detail from the right-hand page of folio 188 of the Book of Kells, the opening page of St Luke's Gospel, which is an elaborate illumination of the word *quoniam*. Some commentators have suggested that the word is given here in the contracted form *qniam*, but the u and o both appear as their Greek equivalents in the yellow diamond, the former as a v, and the latter as a w, presented in a somewhat angular way. The crowd of human figures intermixed with the letters *niam* (lower right) may have been suggested by the words that follow – *multi conati sunt ordinare narrationem*, or 'Forasmuch as many have taken in hand.'

hgeneratio

# St Matthew, Ebbo Gospels

*c.* 816–35 CE **Épernay, France**

**FOLIO** 18 pages (verso) **MATERIALS** Ink and tempera on vellum
**DIMENSIONS** 26 x 21 cm/10⅜ x 8¼ in.

The Ebbo Gospels were made in the 9th century at the atelier, or workshop, of the Benedictine Abbey of Hautvillers for Ebbo, Archbishop of Rheims. This is a Carolingian manuscript, a term named for the Emperor Charlemagne and his dynasty, and was produced during the reign of his son, Louis the Pious. Charlemagne was a great religious reformer and this included patronage of manuscripts. He encouraged artists and scribes to study examples of classical Roman art, especially those associated with Constantine, the first Christian emperor. Carolingian artists depended almost exclusively upon the emperor and his court, including bishops, for their patronage. Nevertheless, not all Carolingian art is the same, with each atelier having different characteristics. The Ebbo Gospels illustrate the general Carolingian trend of trying to produce the naturalistic quality of Roman painting. This is seen here in the attempt to give the figure of Matthew depth with highlights and shadows and to give architectural depth to the book stand and stool. The great energy of this author portrait is characteristic of the Rheims school. The lines, especially those of Matthew's robe, have a distinct liveliness, producing the best example of the 'shivering' or 'frenetic' Rheims style. All the symbols that are common in evangelist author portraits are present here: a depiction of the book that Matthew has written, his writing implements (an ink horn and stylus) and his personal symbol (a winged man in the upper right corner).

## Morgan Gospels

Medieval illuminated Gospel Books adopted the classical idea of an author portrait, including one for each of the four evangelists. This is an example of Luke from the Morgan Gospels.

'For by however much the soul is a more excellent substance than the body, by so much should we treat the care of the soul with more excellent concern than that of the body, just as the Lord teaches in the Gospels, as you well know.'

AGOBARD OF LYONS TO LOUIS THE PIOUS (C. 830)

## Codex Aureus of Freckenhorst

The 11th-century Codex Aureus of Freckenhorst features an example of ivory used in its treasure binding. It is carved with Christ in a mandorla, holding a Gospel Book. Only a few traces of the original jade, turquoise and amethyst remain on the binding.

'And they saw the God of Israel: and there was under his feet as it were a paved work of a sapphire stone, and as it were the body of heaven, in his clearness.'

VULGATE, EXODUS 24:10

# Codex Aureus of Echternach

980 CE Germanisches Nationalmuseum, Nuremberg, Germany

**MATERIALS** Gold, ivory, pearls, gemstones  **LANGUAGE** Latin
**DIMENSIONS** 42 x 33 cm/16 ⅜ x 13 in.

The Gospels hold the stories of Christ's life and death and Gospel Books were therefore some of the most valued medieval codices. They were often lavishly illustrated and made with the highest-quality materials by the most talented hands, often citing Exodus 24:10 as justification. The covers were no exception to this rule and, during the early Middle Ages, it was quite common to find the Gospels enclosed in treasure bindings made of precious metals, gemstones and ivory. Few of these survive, partly because precious metals are relatively easy to melt and reuse, and this happened especially during the chaos of the Viking raids of the 9th and 10th centuries. One of the finest surviving examples, however, is the front cover of the Codex Aureus of Echternach. It is attributed to the Trier workshop set up by Egbert, Archbishop of Trier. The main subject is the Crucifixion of Christ, carved from ivory. This central plaque is surrounded by panels wrought in low relief using repoussé – a metalwork technique whereby a design is hammered from the reverse side. The four reliefs at the top and bottom depict the four Evangelists. The sides show the Virgin Mary (top left) and Saint Peter (top right), standing above the young Emperor Otto III (bottom left) and his mother Theophanu (bottom right). The panels are bordered by a framework of gold filigree, which has been set with gemstones and cloisonné enamel. Thinner gold bands run across the cover diagonally to form an 'X', the letter often used as an abbreviation for Christ.

# Beatus of Liébana, San Millán Codex

10th century CE **Real Academia de la Historia, Madrid, Spain**

**ORIGIN** Monastery of San Millán de la Cogolla, Spain
**AUTHOR** Beatus of Liébana **DIMENSIONS** 36 x 25 cm/14⅛ x 8⅞ in.

## The Damned

Illustrations by Beatus in the San Millán Codex also portrayed the horrors that awaited those who were not among the 144,000. These souls are shown here worshipping the beast and the dragon, as described in the Book of Revelation.

'Then I looked, and behold, on Mount Zion stood the Lamb, and with him 144,000 who had his name and his Father's name written on their foreheads.'

REVELATION 14:1

The early Middle Ages were a period of biblical summary and commentary. This tradition was extended to many books of the Bible as monks, priests and the faithful sought to better understand them. The final book of the New Testament, Revelation, was one of the most important, yet most difficult books to interpret and illustrate. From it comes some of the most important iconography of Christianity, including Christ in Majesty as he judges souls at the end of the world and the four symbols of the Evangelists. In the 8th century, a Spanish monk and theologian named Beatus of Liébana gathered together the Book of Revelation with introductions and commentaries by the best theologians available, including Caesarius of Arles, Augustine of Hippo, Ambrose of Milan, Gregory the Great and Isidore of Seville. This compilation became so important that it is simply known as a Beatus. Beatus manuscripts are one of the preeminent forms of Mozarab art, that which was produced in a Muslim, or Muslim-influenced style, by Christians under Muslim rule. This manuscript is in both the Mozarab and a later style, completed by at least two different hands, most likely because the sacking of the monastery by al-Mansur in the late 10th century forced the production to stop until resources could be gathered to complete it. This scene of the Adoration of the Lamb is one of a total of forty-nine illustrations. It depicts some of the 144,000 saved souls worshipping Christ in the form of the Agnus Dei, or Lamb of God.

## Musical Notation

The Codex Calixtinus is also one of the earliest sources of written music. It contains a two-part polyphony for the matins responsories, which are chants with alternating parts for the cantor and choir for the morning service that ends at dawn.

'Sing joyfully to God with one voice with me in one cry of exultation, because in all my journey he who is mighty has confirmed mercy upon me.'

SAEWULF'S ACCOUNT OF HIS PILGRIMAGE (1102–03)

# Codex Calixtinus

*c.* 1150–60 CE **Santiago de Compostela, Galicia, Spain**

**MATERIALS** Ink on vellum **LANGUAGE** Latin
**FOLIOS** 225 **DIMENSIONS** 29.5 x 21.5 cm/11⅝ x 8⅜ in.

One of the most important aspects of medieval religious life was pilgrimage: to express gratitude, or for healing or penance. After Jerusalem and Rome, the holiest pilgrimage site for medieval Europe was Santiago de Compostela in north-western Spain, where in 813 a bishop was said to have found the burial place of the Apostle James. In the 12th century, the French monk and scholar Aymeric Picaud gathered together a number of manuscripts related to St James and the pilgrimage routes to Santiago, including sermons about James, descriptions of his martyrdom, liturgies, accounts of his miracles, the translation (movement) of his body from Jerusalem to Spain, and the history of Charlemagne and Roland. However, the last portion, a guidebook for pilgrims, is most famous; it notes the best relics to see along the way, describes the local customs and warns which foods to avoid, among other advice. The entire manuscript was originally falsely attributed to Pope Callixtus II, for whom it is named, in order to lend it greater credibility. It even includes a fake letter from Callixtus to Cluny and the archbishop of Compostela. The most well-known copy is the manuscript held at the Cathedral of Santiago de Compostela, with its gorgeous illuminations, such as that seen here of St James offering a blessing. The hand in which it is written is beautifully clear, making this a luxury item despite it being described as the world's first guidebook. This copy was stolen from the cathedral archives in July 2011, but was recovered almost a year to the day later, in July 2012, seemingly unaltered and undamaged, but having achieved greater fame.

# INCIPIT LIBER .IIII. SCI. IACOBI. Apli.

ARGUMENTUM BEATI CALIXTI PP.

Si ueritas apto lectore nris uoluminibus; reqratur
in huius codicis serie. amputato esitacionis scru
pulo secure intelligatur; Que eni in eo scribun
tur; multi adhuc uiuentes uera ee testantur;

## Cap. i.

QVATVOR vie sunt que ad
scm iacobum tendentes in unum ad
pontem regine. in horis yspanie co
adunantur; Alia per scm egidiu
& montem pessulanum. & tholosam. &
portus aspi tendit; alia p scam uia
riam podii. ⁊ scam fidem cocquis. et
scm petrum de moyssaco incedit; alia
p scam mariam magda
lenam uizeliaci. ⁊ scm
leonardum lemouicensem. & urbem petragoricensem pgit;
alia p scm marrinum tyronensem. ⁊ scm ylarium pictauen
sem. & scm iohem angliacensem. & scm eutropium scto
nensem. & urbem burdegalensem uadit; Illa que p scam

La repance repre li
suen de la bataille qi
ont palme com croez
t la fille lumere o les pu
cele alen contra a tim
brez e a cimbel por chan
tet de los e li perte la
inguarde de si e arrez
rolanz t si se repent
de son uou.

Ce que repre e repance
ce qe uenqui la bataille
seue feu feu det qi apl
sa resurrection uenqui
ce de la mort t despri
le deable la fille qe li e
uenue contra a timbal
sea a cimbel par lui fere
ione seue la synagogue
qui uent deuant thu
crist t li feroit de ch
sel recumnadu e ce fu
de denanz e de chas

Ce la sacre seu repre sa
fille e li e fere doul
par cele lumere en e
fu blande e laurre
fu noire

Ce qe repre sacma la
fille iurnise sonpa mele
ne par ne fu blande
noire seue feu crist qe li
certia la synagogue e en
seir doul par cele lume fu
noire e par blande la
blande seue sa crist
ra a lacrme e ce fu
noir seue le gereu e qi
ne uelent en la uoir
ant lum deuant e de est
aurez de la mescrance e
tez de la crance

Se marie la pncele
le deuant somp
re qui estre ians e o
uroz t li dit dome
ne respere soueroe
me puccle t qil su ferc
t ele repance a ses pu
celes

Ce qe la puccle respre
de lame seue la
synagogue qi dema
da al resture respre
de sa me e si li done
ele le reume a bur
sel e au deu t terr
rien

La descent nul an
glese paroleau
ne uielle e li dit tu
conceuroz un enfint
qi sera mule fors qi
aura nom sanson
e cele sen esturcuit la

Ce qe li angles parla
en marion a la sa
me t li dist un conceue
ra un enfant mult sor
qi aura nom sanson
seue le sepme t lange qi
uient la sa une e lui
annunca la salue e li edi
annuncameuant un estre
qi sera mult granz t
mult forz t lauta uie
uient

# Bible Moralisée

*c.* 1220–30 CE  **Osterreichische Nationalbibliothek, Vienna, Austria**

**ORIGIN** Paris, France  **DIMENSIONS** 34.5 x 26 cm/13½ x 10¼ in.
**MATERIALS** Ink and gold on vellum  **LANGUAGE** Old French

In the 13th century a new type of religious book, known as
the *Bible moralisée*, appeared in France. These were not complete
Bibles, but instead had selections of carefully paired Old and New
Testament scenes, complete with commentary and interpretation.
They were sumptuously illustrated and gilded, and among the
most expensive medieval manuscripts to produce; consequently
they were commissioned solely by French queens and kings. One
of the first, if not the first, *Bible moralisée*, now known as Vienna
2554, was probably commissioned by Blanche of Castile, the wife
of King Louis VIII. The large number of illuminations showing
childbirth underline a mother's connection to her son, a fact that
Blanche, who was regent twice for her son Louis IX, would have
wanted to emphasize. It has also been suggested that Blanche
intended the book be used as part of her son's education, making
it a religious version of the 'mirrors for princes' genre of medieval
literature intended to instruct kings. Vienna 2554 has survived,
but with missing pages and other pages out of order. Each page
has eight image medallions. The bottom four images of Folio 61v
shown here include two Old Testament scenes from Judges at
the top, showing Jephthah sacrificing his daughter and an angel
announcing the birth of Samson to his mother. Each of the bottom
medallions offers a New Testament parallel or commentary for
the image above it. On the left is Christ splitting 'Synagoga' – a
personification of Judaism – in two, making the 'unfaithful' Jews
and the 'faithful' Christians. On the right is a New Testament
annunciation scene.

### Architect of the World

The frontispiece of Vienna
2554 is one of the most famous
medieval illustrations. It shows
God creating the world, but as an
architect or craftsman, complete
with a pair of compasses.

'Guided by the holy
nurture and sound
doctrine of so pious a
mother, our Louis began
to develop as a boy of
outstanding talent…and
to seek the Lord.'

GEOFFREY OF BEAULIEU,
BIOGRAPHER OF LOUIS IX

# Hereford Mappa Mundi

*c.* 1285–1300 CE  **Hereford Cathedral, England, UK**

**SIGNED** Richard of Haldingham and Lafford (Richard de Bello)
**MATERIALS** Ink on vellum   **DIMENSIONS** 158 x 133 cm/62¼ x 52⅜ in.

One of the most common types of map during the Middle Ages was the mappa mundi or map of the world. The largest surviving example is the one currently on display at Hereford Cathedral in England. Although by the 13th century far more accurate maps were available, the existence of around 1,100 surviving mappae mundi attests to their great popularity. This was because of their symbolic importance; they illustrate how medieval scholars interpreted the world spiritually, as well as geographically. The Hereford example is a TO mappa mundi, a term derived from the O shape of the map and the T shape formed by the Mediterranean and Nile. TO maps, like most mappae mundi, placed the East and Asia at the top, with Africa on the lower right and Europe on the lower left. This configuration allowed Jerusalem – the holiest city in the medieval Christian world – to be placed in the centre of the map. The central point was carefully calculated, as can be seen by the small perforation made by a compass that is still visible in the centre where Jerusalem was positioned. Other religious images are also included: Christ in Majesty (above the circle of the map); Eden (a small circle at the top of the map); Noah's ark; the Tower of Babel; and the Red Sea, together with the route taken by Moses in the Book of Exodus. In all, the map depicts more than 400 towns, 15 biblical events, 33 plants and animals, as well as several classical scenes. The map shows some signs of wear, especially Hereford itself, which has been dulled by the many pointing fingers, and the city of Paris, which was scratched through at some point.

### Farum Brigantium

Farum Brigantium is an ancient Roman lighthouse on the Galician coast of Spain. The 55-metre (180-ft) tall tower was used to guide ships in the Atlantic, including religious pilgrims travelling by sea to Santiago de Compostela. Since the 20th century, it has been known as the Tower of Hercules and is the oldest existing lighthouse in the world.

'The inhabited mass of solid land is called round after the roundness of a circle, because it is like a wheel.'

ISIDORE OF SEVILLE, *ETYMOLOGIAE* (7TH CENTURY)

# Bohun Psalter

c. 1356–73 CE  **British Library, London, England, UK**

**COMMISSIONED BY** Bohun Family  **MATERIALS** Ink on parchment
**DIMENSIONS** 34 x 23.5 cm/13⅜ x 9½ in.

### The Raising of Lazarus

Psalters often included events from the four Gospel Books of the New Testament, such as the story of Christ resurrecting Lazarus from the dead, one of the most prominent miracles attributed to Jesus in the Gospel of John. Jesus restores Lazarus of Bethany to life four days after his death. The story has also been a popular subject for artists throughout history, including Albrecht Dürer in 1512.

'Save me, O God: for the waters are come in even unto my soul.'

PSALM 68:1

Although the Gospel Book was the most lavishly illustrated book of the early Middle Ages, the high and later Middle Ages were dominated by the psalter, a book that was a combination of the Book of Psalms and other devotional material. First developed in the West in around the 8th century, psalters had become common by the 11th century. The Bohun Psalter is an elaborate example of a psalter in Gothic script, which was commissioned by a member of the Bohun family, either one of the earls or Mary de Bohun, the first wife of Henry IV of England. The Bohun family arms are included in at least four different places in the manuscript, which places its production in Essex, where the family sponsored a workshop at Pleshey Castle that is credited with the production of at least ten manuscripts. This psalter has fifteen very large historiated initials, including the one shown here. The S begins Psalm 68, which in Latin is *Salvum me fac Deus* (translating as 'please God save me'). The scene around the S shows the Ark of the Covenant being brought to Jerusalem and King David, to whom the authorship of the Psalms are attributed. The Psalms are praises to God, which lend themselves to personal devotion and help explain the popularity of psalters. The Bohun Psalter also includes a feast calendar with saints days, canticles (biblical songs of praise not from the Psalms), the Hours of the Virgin (liturgy) and other prayers. Psalters were intended for laypeople who wanted to increase their personal devotion by partially following aspects of monastic life in their secular lives, but who could not, or did not want to, join a monastery or convent.

al
uit
me
fac
deus
quo
nia
intr
uerūt
aque
usq;
ad

animam meam · ꝉ nfirus sum in limo p
fundi: et non est substancia · ꝉ eni in alti
tudinem maris: et tempestas demersit me.
Laboraui clamans: rauce facte sunt fauces
mee: defecerunt oculi mei dum spero in deum
meum · ꝉ ultiplicati sunt super capillos
capitis mei: qui oderunt me gratis · Confor
tati sunt qui persecuti sunt me inimici mei in
iuste: que non rapui tunc exsoluebam · De
us tu scis insipienciam meam: et delicta me
a a te non sunt abscondita · Non erubescat
in me qui expectant te domine: domine uir

# Chained Library

15th century CE **Zutphen, Netherlands**

**ORIGIN** Netherlands  **FOUNDED BY** Conrad Slindewater, Herman Berner
**STYLE** Gothic  **SIZE OF COLLECTION** 750 books

As the demand for access to books increased in the late Middle Ages, the foundations such as monasteries and universities that owned collections searched for ways to make them accessible yet secure. One of the solutions created was the chained library, in which books could be connected to lecterns and bookshelves by metal bars and chains. This allowed easy use without constant supervision or inviting theft. The oldest intact library, with original chains, furniture and books, is the Zutphen Library. St Walburga's Church, one of the largest in the Netherlands, was built in the 11th century, but in the 16th century its twelve canons (clerics) had developed a large library, in part because they served as legal advisers to the Duke of Guelders and the town council. To house these books, churchwardens Conrad Slindewater and Herman Berner planned a library, which was built above the vestry, following the curved shape of the apse and ambulatory. Slindewater's records reveal that he intended the library to be a bulwark against the Reformation, which was rapidly gaining momentum, and one that would contain works to counteract it. To this end, sixty keys to the library's door were given to the canons and some of the townspeople, to ensure access. The distance between each lectern in the public reading room is 0.8 metres (2⅝ ft), which together with ample light from large windows made the room an inviting place to read and study. The collection includes Bible commentaries, saints' lives, legal works and classical works. Five of the books are manuscripts and eighty-five are incunabula, books printed before 1500.

## Hereford Chained Library

The chained library at Hereford Cathedral is one of the most famous examples in England. It houses more than 220 manuscripts, including the 8th-century Hereford Gospels, and was constructed in the 17th century. It is the largest surviving chained library in Europe, with all its chains, rods and locks intact. The books are shelved with their page edges facing out (rather than their spines), allowing the reader to take down the book and open it without having to turn it round and therefore avoids getting it tangled up in the book's chain.

> 'I have always imagined that Paradise will be a kind of library.'
>
> JORGE LUIS BORGES, WRITER

## Annunciation to Joachim

The Marian theme is continued on the opposite page to Catherine of Cleves praying to the Virgin. It shows Joachim, the Virgin's father, receiving the announcement from the angel Gabriel that his wife Anne is with child. After many years of childlessness, Mary's parents had given up all hope of having a child. The rabbits to the left of the miniature symbolize the returned fertility of the barren couple.

> 'O Mary, you embody,
> all God taught to our race,
> For you are first and
> foremost, In fullness
> of His grace.'

MORNING PRAYER,
HOURS OF THE VIRGIN

# The Hours of Catherine of Cleves

C. 1440 CE **Morgan Library, New York, USA**

**ARTIST** Master of Catherine of Cleves    **MATERIALS** Ink and gold on vellum
**LANGUAGE** Latin    **DIMENSIONS** 19.2 x 13 cm/7½ x 5⅛ in.

In the late Middle Ages, books of hours became the focus of personal devotion. They contained the devotional texts of a psalter, but without the complete Book of Psalms. Books of hours were frequently made for women of high and middle status, and this one was commissioned for Catherine of Cleves by her father or husband upon her marriage to Arnold of Egmond, Duke of Guelders in 1430, although it was so elaborately illuminated that it was not finished for another decade. The result is considered to be the finest example of Dutch manuscript illumination, with more than 100 elaborate miniatures by an anonymous artist who was clearly influenced by contemporaries such as Jan van Eyck. It opens with a full-page illumination of Catherine praying from her book to the Virgin and Child. This demonstrates the artist's characteristic style, which features elaborate borders with birds and botanical elements, and a naturalistically detailed, black and white tiled floor under the Virgin's feet. At the heart of the book are the Hours of the Virgin – a set of psalms, hymns, biblical readings and divine offices for the eight hours of the day: matins (night), lauds (upon rising), prime (early morning), terce (mid morning), sext (noon), nones (mid afternoon), vespers (early evening) and compline (before retiring). These offices provided a devout woman with the proper devotion for each time of day. In the 19th century the manuscript was unbound and its pages were shuffled before it was rebound into the two volumes that exist today.

# The Gutenberg Bible

1450–59 CE **Mainz, Germany**

**CREATED BY** Johannes Gutenberg **MATERIALS** Ink on paper and vellum
**LANGUAGE** Latin **DIMENSIONS** 30.7 x 44.5 cm/12⅛ x 17½ in.

### Binding

Nine of the known copies have their original bindings, most of which are of German origin. Most copies were bound in two volumes, although some were bound in three or four.

'A true intimacy cemented by Christ Himself is ... one such as ours, wrought by a common fear of God and a joint study of the divine scriptures.'

ST JEROME,
LETTER TO PAULINUS

When German publisher Johannes Gutenberg printed a run of 160 to 185 Bibles in the mid 15th century, it was groundbreaking not simply because he was printing, but because he was using moveable type, instead of carving or etching a plate for each page. He had invented moveable type and produced the first major printed book in the West. In fact, the Gutenberg Bible had more ties to what came before it than it did revolutionary breaks with the past. The text itself is the Vulgate, the Latin translation made by St Jerome in the late 4th century. Gutenberg even kept the traditional Latin abbreviations used by medieval scribes. Furthermore, while around three-quarters of the books were printed on Italian paper, the remaining quarter was printed on vellum, the material used throughout the Middle Ages for codices. When paper was used, it was 'double folio' printing, where one sheet was printed with two pages on each side. Gutenberg Bibles vary widely, not only because of what they were printed on, but because they were sold unbound and undecorated. After finding it too difficult to run the pages through the printing press twice to be rubricated, these title areas were left blank and each had to be carefully hand lettered in red, as well as illustrated. The entire run of books sold out almost immediately, with purchases made almost entirely for religious institutions as far away as England and even possibly Sweden and Hungary. Forty-eight complete or substantial copies of the Gutenberg Bible are known to survive, including this beautifully illuminated example of the opening page, the letter of St Jerome to Paulinus that served as the preface to the edition.

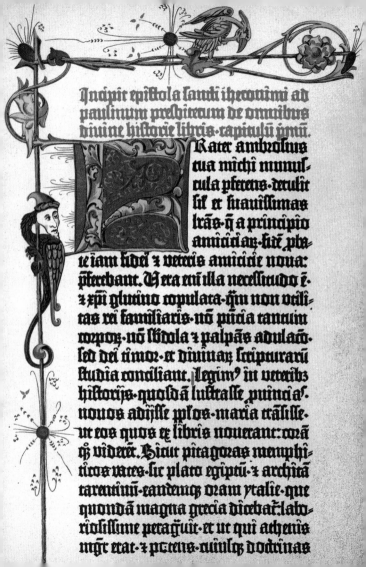

Incipit epiſtola ſancti iheronimi ad
paulinum presbiterum de omnibus
diuine hiſtorie libris · capitulu pmu ·

Rater ambroſius
tua michi munuſ
cula pferens · detulit
ſil' et ſuauiſſimas
lras · q̃ a principio
amiciciaꝛ · fidi ꝓba
te iam fidei ⁊ veteris amicicie noua:
ꝓferebant. Vera eni illa neceſſitudo e̅ ·
⁊ xp̃i glutino copulata · qua non vtili
tas rei familiaris · nõ pñcia tantum
corpoꝝ · nõ ſͤbdola ⁊ palpãs adulacõ
ſed dei timor · et diuinaꝛ ſcripturaru̅
ſtudia conciliant. legim⁹ in veterib⁹
hiſtoriis · quoſdã luſtraſſe puincias ·
nouos adiiſſe ppl̃os · maria trãſiſſe ·
ut eos quos ex libris nouerant: coram
q̃ viderent. Sicut pitagoras memphi
ticos vates · ſic plato egiptu̅ · ⁊ architã
tarentinu̅ · eande̅q; oram ytalie · que
quondã magna grecia dicebaꞇ: labo
rioſiſſime peragrauit · et ut qui atheniſ
mgr̃ erat · ⁊ potens · cuiuſꝗ doctrinas

Sieben köpffe Martini Luthers
Vom Hochwürdigen Sacrament des Altars / Durch
Doctor Jo. Cocleus.

# Ninety-Five Theses

1517 CE **Wittenberg, Saxony, Germany**

**ORIGIN** Wittenberg, Saxony    **AUTHOR** Martin Luther
**FIRST PRINTED** Germany    **ORIGINAL LANGUAGE** Latin

The invention of moveable type and the rise of the printing press in the 15th century marked the beginning of a more significant change in the relationship between religion and the written word. In 1517 the Augustinian friar and theology professor Martin Luther wrote *Disputatio pro declaratione virtutis indulgentiarum*, better known as Ninety-Five Theses on the Power and Efficacy of Indulgences. Contrary to popular belief, there is no strong evidence to support the claim that Luther actually nailed the theses to a church door in Wittenberg; however, it is certain that he distributed his ninety-five objections to the university community there in 1517. Written in Latin – the language of clerics, law and universities – Luther intended the theses to spark theological and academic debate. He was particularly concerned about the selling of indulgences (payments for the remission of sins) by the Catholic Church in order to finance the rebuilding of St Peter's Basilica in Rome. Luther's intention was reform; however, the printing press quickly spread the theses and provoked widespread religious debate. In 1517 three editions of around 300 copies were made of the theses in Leipzig, Nuremberg and Basel. Within weeks they were translated into German and spread even faster, not only across German-speaking areas, but throughout much of Europe. The printed version of Luther's theses is an excellent example of how printing changed not only the form of the book, but also the way in which theological ideas were formulated and spread. The Ninety-Five Theses are widely believed to have sparked the beginning of the Protestant Reformation.

## Counter-Reformation

As the Protestant Reformation gained momentum, Martin Luther gave up on reform and organized a separate Protestant church. The Counter-Reformation adapted the printing press to its own ends, as seen by this 16th-century anti-Luther pamphlet depicting him as a seven-headed creature.

'Out of love and zeal for clarifying the truth, these items written below will be debated at Wittenberg.'

MARTIN LUTHER,
NINETY-FIVE THESES

AMORE ET STVDIO ELVCIDANDAE
ueritatis hæc subscripta disputabunt Vuittenbergæ, Præsidête
R.P. Martino Luther, Artiû & S. Theologiæ Magistro, eius-
demq; ibidem lectore Ordinatio. Quare petit ut qui non pos-
sunt uerbis præsentes nobiscum disceptare, agant id literis ab-
sentes. In nomine domini nostri Iesu Christi. Amen.

i   Ominus & Magister noster Iesus Christus, di-
cendo pœnitentia agite &c. omnem uitam fi-
delium, pœnitentiam esse uoluit.

ij   Quod uerbû pœnitentia de pœnitentia sacra-
mentali (.i. confessionis & satisfactionis quæ
sacerdotum ministerio celebratur) non potest intelligi.

iij  Non tamen sola intêdit interiore: immo interior nulla est, nisi
foris operetur uarias carnis mortificationes.

iiij  Manet itaq; pœna donec manet odium sui (.i. pœnitentia uera
intus) scilicet usq; ad introitum regni cælorum.

v   Papa non uult nec potest, ullas pœnas remittere: præter eas,
quas arbitrio uel suo uel canonum imposuit.

vj  Papa nô potest remittere ullam culpâ, nisi declarâdo & appro-
bando remissam a deo. Aut certe remittêdo casus reseruatos
sibi, quibus contêptis culpa prorsus remaneret.

vij  Nulli prorsus remittit deus culpam, quin simul eum subijciat
humiliatum in omnibus sacerdoti suo uicario.

viij  Canones pœnitentiales solû uiuentibus sunt impositi: nihilq;
morituris, secundû eosdem debet imponi.

ix  Inde bene nobis facit spiritussanctus in Papa: excipiêdo in su-
is decretis semper articulum mortis & necessitatis.

x   Indocte & male faciût sacerdotes ij, qui morituris pœnitêtias
canonicas in purgatorium reseruant.

xj  Zizania illa de mutanda pœna Canonica in pœnâ purgatorij, uidentur certe dormientibus Episcopis seminata.

xij  Olim pœnæ canonicæ nô post, sed ante absolutionem impo-
nebantur, tanq; tentamenta ueræ contritionis.

xiij  Morituri, per mortem omnia
tui iam sunt, habentes iure e

xiiij  Imperfecta sanitas seu charita
magnû timorem, tâtoq; mai

xv  Hic timor & horror, satis est,
nam purgatorij, cum sit pro

xvj  Videntur, infernus, purgator
ratio, prope desperatio, secu

xvij  Necessarium uidetur animab
rorem, ita augeri charitatem

xviij  Nec probatû uidetur ullis, au
extra statum meriti seu aug

xix  Nec hoc probatû esse uidetu
& securæ, saltem oês, licet n

xx  Igit Papa per remissionê ple
citer omniû intelligit, sed a s

xxj  Errant itaq; indulgentiarû pra
pæ indulgentias, homine ab

xxij  Quin nullam remittit animab
ta debuissent secundum Ca

xxiij  Si remissio ulla omniû omni
est eam nô nisi perfectissim

xxiiij  Falli ob id necesse est, maiore
illam & magnificam pœna

xxv  Qualê potestatê habet Papa
glibet Episcopus & curat'in

i  Optime facit Papa, q; nô pot
sed per modum suffragij, dat

ij  Hominê prædicant, qui stati
nierit, euolare dicunt anima

iij  Certû est nûmo in cistam tin
ciam posse: suffragiû aût ecc

iiij  Quis scit si omnes animæ in p
Sancto Seuerino & paschali

v  Nullus securus est de ueritate

6 Holy Objects

# Bewcastle Cross

*c.* 7th century CE  **St Cuthbert's Church, Bewcastle, Cumbria, UK**

**MATERIAL** Stone  **HEIGHT** 4.5 m/15 ft
**DIMENSIONS AT BASE** 56 x 54 cm/22 x 21¼ in.

The Bewcastle Cross, also known as the Bewcastle Monument, is one of two early Anglo-Saxon crosses that are the largest and most elaborately decorated examples to have survived (the other being the Ruthwell Cross in Scotland). While there is some scholarly disagreement on dating the Bewcastle Cross, most put its carving and installation in the early 8th century, the era of Bede. While only the shaft remains, it is safe to assume that it was once a complete cross because of the dowel hole on top that would have been used to attach another piece of stone. The remaining shaft is still where it was first installed in the churchyard of St Cuthbert's Church. It is ornately carved on all four sides. The western side, has the figural elements, including John the Baptist at the top and Christ treading on the beasts while holding a spear or staff, a version of the resurrected Christ in Triumph. Below the figure of Christ is a falconer, generally identified as St John the Evangelist. The other three sides contain knotwork, geometrical patterns, a sundial and animal figures. Also engraved in the stone are runic inscriptions featuring the names Cyneburch and Alcfrith, an Anglo-Saxon queen and her king. It is quite likely that the Bewcastle Cross served both secular and religious functions. This can be seen in its role as a marker of royal remembrance and the idea of the triumph of memory over death. Its rather martial depiction of Christ also places it firmly in an Anglo-Saxon royal context as it reveals imagery from the New Testament that would have resonated with the elites of a culture whose pre-conversion gods were warlike and physically strong.

## Ruthwell Cross

While the contemporary Anglo-Saxon stone cross at Ruthwell in Dumfriesshire, Scotland has many similarities, including a depiction of Christ treading on beasts, it has more religious imagery, such as this depiction of Mary Magdalene at Christ's feet. The Ruthwell Cross was smashed by iconoclasts in 1642 and lay in the churchyard until it was restored in the 19th century by Scottish minister Henry Duncan.

'The crosses of Bewcastle and Ruthwell...are the greatest achievement of their date in the whole of Europe.'

NIKOLAUS PEVSNER,
ARCHITECTURAL HISTORIAN

# Plaque with Christ in Majesty and the Four Evangelists

1000–1100 CE  **Metropolitan Museum of Art, New York, USA**

**ORIGIN** Ottonian Germany  **MATERIAL** Ivory
**DIMENSIONS** 15.6 x 9.5 cm / 6 ⅛ x 3 ¾ in.

This ivory plaque was created in a workshop in Ottonian Germany, most probably in Cologne. It is made up of three ivory strips and depicts the common theme of the enthroned Christ on Judgement Day, surrounded by the four Evangelists and their symbols, as described in the New Testament. The figures have great energy – Christ's hand and feet overlap the edge of the border of his mandorla (almond-shaped panel) and each Evangelist interacts with his symbol. It is possible that this plaque was originally meant to adorn a treasure binding for a copy of the Gospels. However, its current attachment to a 15th-century lectionary is equally important. Lectionaries are books that match the liturgical calendar with readings from the Bible for use in liturgy and sermons. Catholic lectionaries originated around the 6th century when popes, such as Leo I and Gregory the Great, realized that the classical oratory tradition and Greek were becoming lost. They began recording proper verses for each Sunday and major feast days, such as Christmas and All Saints' Day, that were not Sundays. After being formalized in the Carolingian era, they came to include three years' of readings, with one year each dedicated to Matthew, Mark and Luke, and John being read during Easter and Lent. Secondary readings were included, generally from the New Testament epistles of St Paul, which caused late medieval lectionaries to expand to three or four volumes. Similar Byzantine lectionaries were also developed by the 8th century.

## The Lovell Lectionary

The Lovell Lectionary, also from the 15th century, was an English version commissioned by John, Lord Lovell of Titchmarsh. He gave it to Salisbury Cathedral in order to garner prayers from the canons there for himself and his wife, Maud de Holand. The artist who illuminated the lectionary was John Siferwas, a Dominican friar who worked on other books, including the Sherborne Missal.

'Nothing is so characteristic of medieval preaching as the fact that it was fundamentally shaped by the lectionary.'

HUGHES OLIPHANT OLD, PROFESSOR OF THEOLOGY

# Chalice of Doña Urraca

11th century CE **Basilica of San Isidro, Léon, Spain**

**COMMISSIONED BY** Fernando I, Doña Urraca
**MATERIALS** Agate, gold, onyx, precious stones

## Holy Chalice of Valencia

The Vatican has never endorsed any chalice as the Holy Grail, although the Holy Chalice of Valencia has been venerated by both Pope John Paul II and Pope Benedict XVI. The most ancient part of the chalice is the cup of polished brown agate, which archaeologists have dated back to around 100 BCE.

'The cup, the cup itself, from which our Lord, Drank at the last sad supper with his own.'

ALFRED, LORD TENNYSON, *IDYLLS OF THE KING* (1859–85)

The Chalice of Doña Urraca is made of two Roman cups. In the 11th century, these were given by a Fatimid caliph in Cairo to a Muslim emir in Al-Andalus (Muslim Spain), who then gave them as a gift to King Fernando I of León. Fernando in turn gave the cups to his daughter Urraca. Urraca or her father had the two cups joined together and lined with gold, then set with precious stones, pearls and a small white face made of glass paste. At the joint between the cups is an elaborate knot, underneath which is a filigree inscription that reads: 'In the Name of God, Urraca [daughter] of Fernando.' Chalices are of great importance to Christians because of their role in the sacrament of the Eucharist. Chalices are used either to symbolize the Last Supper or as a vessel to hold the wine that is transubstantiated, literally turned into the blood of Christ. This chalice, however, is not only very old and valuable, but Margarita Torres and José Ortega del Rio claimed in their book *The Kings of the Grail* published in 2014 that it is the Holy Grail, the actual cup from which Christ drank wine at the Last Supper. They base their claim on the provenance of the cups, as well as the fact that the original cups date to the time of Christ. They say they have traced the origins of the chalice to the early Christian communities in Jerusalem. While the initial reaction of scholars has been sceptical, the small treasury museum at the Basilica of San Isidro where the Chalice of Doña Urraca is housed has been besieged with so many people coming to view it that they have been forced to remove it from display until they can arrange for a larger exhibition space.

# Baptismal Font

1107–18 CE  **Church of Saint-Barthelemy, Liège, Belgium**

**COMMISSIONED BY** Father Hellin   **ARTIST** Attributed to Renier de Huy
**MATERIAL** Copper alloy   **DIAMETER** 91 cm/36 in.

## Mosan Masterpiece

The Shrine of the Three Kings, a reliquary at Cologne Cathedral, is considered the high point of Mosan art. Created by French goldsmith Nicholas of Verdun, it features elaborate gold sculptures of the prophets and apostles.

'Baptism is the initiatory sign by which we are admitted to the fellowship of the church, that being engrafted into Christ we may be accounted children of God.'

JOHN CALVIN, *INSTITUTES OF THE CHRISTIAN RELIGION* 4.15.1

Shared by almost all forms of Christianity, baptism is one of the earliest and most enduring Christian sacraments. The sacrament involves either bodily immersion in a font or the sprinkling of water upon the head. The form of the sacrament comes from the Gospel accounts that describe Christ's cousin, John the Baptist, baptizing his followers in the River Jordan and then Christ asking to be baptized as well. The centrality of baptism to Christianity has led to scenes of baptism being portrayed in countless illustrated Bibles, frescoes, sculptures and paintings. Naturally, it is a subject that frequently makes an appearance on baptismal fonts themselves. The baptismal font at the Church of Saint-Barthelemy in Liège, Belgium was originally commissioned for Notre-Dame-aux-Fonts, a small church used as the city's baptistery. It is described in the Liège Rhyming Chronicle, but without the artist's name. Its most common attribution, to Renier de Huy, would make it a product of the Mosan Romanesque tradition (Mosan was a regional art style from the Meuse valley in present-day Belgium, Netherlands and Germany). However, it has an unusually classical style for its time period, which has led some to believe it may have been crafted in Rome or Byzantium. Its decorative scheme features the often-depicted baptism of Jesus and other less well-known scenes featuring John the Baptist or baptism, including John preaching, John baptizing followers and Peter baptizing Cornelius. Although the font's original cover was lost, the font itself was safely hidden during the French Revolution and then moved to Saint-Barthelemy in 1804 where it is still in use today.

# Architectural Frieze

1125–50 CE **Metropolitan Museum, New York, USA**

**ORIGIN** Burgundy, France   **MATERIAL** Limestone
**DIMENSIONS** 29 x 56 x 22 cm/11½ x 22 x 8¾ in.

The Christian Church has long led the way in architectural innovation. During the Middle Ages such innovations included ribbed vaulting and flying buttresses. Yet, there were many Roman inheritances underlying this religious architectural form, such as the basilica plan itself. Some Roman architectural details continued well into the Middle Ages. One of these is the frieze – a horizontal carved beam that is generally found in churches under the tympana or running above colonnades or arcades. As they were carved in stone, they reached their pinnacle of popularity within Romanesque churches. When the Gothic style came into fashion, its demand for more windows crowded out many, but not all, of the friezes. The large fragment of a much longer frieze seen here is from a double-sided example, with a simpler design of rosettes and a horizontal moulding on the back. The front of the frieze draws upon both Roman and Christian elements. The rosettes are a classic Roman theme while the cityscape above the four arches includes a medieval scene of chapels, crenellated towers, arcades, tiled roofs and stone. This is appropriate subject matter for a fragment believed to have been a part of the enormous Cluny III church and monastery complex that was virtually destroyed during the iconoclasm of the French Revolution. Cluny, with its direct allegiance to the Pope, St Peter and Rome, would have approved of the emphasis on Roman elements as well as the religious aspects. Scientific testing of trace elements has further matched the frieze to the abbey church at Cluny, eliminating almost all doubt.

## Lincoln Cathedral

One of the most famous English Romanesque friezes is at Lincoln Cathedral. It begins with the creation story (pictured here) and ends with the blessed and the damned. The frieze is thought to date from the time of Bishop Alexander of Lincoln, who held office from 1123 to 1148. It originally adorned the west front of the exterior, but has been moved inside to the Chapel of St James for conservation. A carved copy has been put in its place on the cathedral's west facade.

'Cluniac identity was a mirror of Rome.'

DOMINIQUE IOGNA-PRAT, HISTORIAN

# Arm Reliquary of the Apostles

*c.* 1190 CE  **Cleveland Museum of Art, Ohio, USA**

**COMMISSIONED BY**  Duke Henry the Lion of Saxony    **MATERIALS**  Gilt silver, oak, enamel    **DIMENSIONS**  51 x 14 x 9.2 cm/20¼ x 5½ x 3⅝ in.

### Dalmatic

The reliquary gets its name from the portrait medallions of Christ and the Apostles that line the upper and lower edges of the dalmatic – the long, wide-sleeved tunic still worn as a liturgical vestment by deacons. The dalmatic was introduced by Pope Sylvester I in the 4th century.

'It was a tangible expression of the saint himself.'

STEPHEN FLIEGEL, CURATOR, CLEVELAND MUSEUM OF ART

Relics have been at the heart of Roman Catholic and Eastern Orthodox devotion for centuries. Believing that saints can act as intercessors for them, Christians venerate the relics of saints in hope of a miracle or other answer to their prayers. When Emperor Constantine made Christianity legal in Rome, the underground veneration of biblical and martyr saints spread quickly, with visitors to their graves often removing pieces of the body, clothing or other contact relics as a kind of souvenir of the dead. The demand for relics grew rapidly in the 8th century when they became necessary to the consecration of new altars in the West. Relics were also the ultimate reason for pilgrimages. Such precious objects deserved the best that artisans had to offer when reliquaries were made to hold them. In the 12th century the form of a 'speaking' or shaped reliquary – often shaped as the body part it contained – gained popularity. This relic has been shown by X-ray to be an ulna bone, but belonging to which saint is unknown. It is thought to be one of the Apostles because of the busts decorating it. The reliquary, which originated in Lower Saxony, Germany, is made of champlevé enamelling, gilt silver and hollowed oak. It was commissioned by Duke Henry the Lion, who was given multiple saints' arms on the return journey of his pilgrimage to the Holy Land in 1173. The arm shape allows the bishop who carries it in processions to bless the faithful with the reliquary, which is 'dressed' in a dalmatic (liturgical vestment).

## Diptych of Stilicho

The Diptych of Stilicho is a late Roman example of an ivory diptych. It is held in Monza Cathedral in the Lombardy region of Italy. From the late 4th-century, it depicts Stilicho, his wife Serena (a niece of the Emperor Theodosius) and their son Eucherius. Half Vandal (Germanic), Flavius Stilicho was a high-ranking general whom historian Edward Gibbon described as 'the last of the Roman generals'.

'Frequently ivory diptychs contained certain essential narrative scenes that embodied the polarities of the Christian experience.'

ROBERT G. CALKINS, ACADEMIC

# Diptych of Last Judgement and Coronation of Virgin

*c.* 1250–70 CE **Metropolitan Museum of Art, New York, USA**

**ORIGIN** French   **MATERIALS** Elephant ivory with metal mounts
**DIMENSIONS (OPENED)** 12.7 x 13 x 2 cm / 5 x 5⅛ x ¾ in.

Diptychs are any two flat plates attached by a hinge, but their history is much more nuanced. In classical Rome diptychs were shallow boxes with elaborately carved outer surfaces and wax filling the inner cavities. The wax could be written on with a stylus then melted when the notes were no longer needed and a new surface was desired. The most grand Roman examples were traditionally made to celebrate a new consul's election. By the central Middle Ages, diptychs were frequently still created in ivory, although equally often they were painted panels. A noteworthy change was their new religious purpose as a devotional object, a sort of portable mini-altar. The French example shown here is particularly fine. On the left is the Coronation of the Virgin, attended by a Christ who looks like an earthly French king. Below them is another register with medieval figures, including a king, a bishop and a deacon, who have just received the good news that they are to be saved. This scene of hope is countered on the right by one of dread. Christ in Majesty is enthroned for the Last Judgement, framed by the Virgin Mary and St John. Below are the souls that have been reawakened for the afterlife on the left while those on the right face the Mouth of Hell. The wounds that Christ shows his mother and John underscore the sombre mood. The beautiful high relief sculpting adds not only quality to the diptych, but dramatic emotion consistent with the courtly culture of the 13th century.

# Medieval Pilgrim Badge from Amiens

*c.* 1300 CE  **Perth Museum and Gallery, Scotland, UK**

**ORIGIN** Amiens, France    **ARTIST** Not known
**DIAMETER** 5 cm/2 in.    **MATERIAL** Lead

### St John the Baptist

John the Baptist is one of the most important figures in the life of Jesus. Described as Jesus' cousin in Luke, John appears in all four Gospel books as the one who prepared the way for Christ and then baptized him.

'I, indeed, baptize you with water; but there is coming one more powerful than I, and I am not fit even to unfasten his sandals.'

ST JOHN THE BAPTIST, AS TOLD IN LUKE 3:16

This circular badge, featuring the head of St John the Baptist, was the sign worn by pilgrims to show that they had visited the Cathedral of Amiens in France, where the relic of St John's head was placed in 1207. Each pilgrimage site had its own theme for its badges, for example, a scallop shell for Santiago de Compostela in Spain or St Peter's keys for Rome, which it sold as souvenirs. Most pilgrims, however, could not afford such a long journey and instead frequented local, closer shrines. A database of 108 badges kept by the British Museum in London bears this out; two are from Rome whereas the majority of them come from Canterbury. Popular from 1200 to 1600, the badges were made in large quantities from lead, which meant they were affordable by most people. Badges were made for different types of wear; some had pins, others were worn as pendants, while others still, such as this one, had four rings to enable the badge to be sewn onto clothing. Badges were part of the pilgrim's garb, which also included a coarse tunic, wooden staff and a large hat. Most pilgrim badges have been discovered either in graves or in water, especially around bridges over rivers, such as the Thames. Although many medieval pilgrim badges survive, this one is in particularly good condition with its four rings intact, reverse image of the cross and inscription identifying it as the sign of John the Baptist. This badge has particular meaning for Perth, where it is held in a museum collection, as John the Baptist is its patron saint.

# Pyx

15th century CE  **Musée Cluny, Paris, France**

**ORIGIN** Southern France or northern Spain  **ARTIST** Not known
**MATERIAL** Silver gilt  **DIMENSIONS** 8 x 8.5 cm / 3 x 3¼ in.

### Byzantine Ivory Pyx

An ancient or medieval pyx could be made from a range of materials, from luxurious ones such as enamel or ivory to more mundane ones such as cork or wood. This elaborately carved ivory pyx from 6th-century Byzantium features scenes from the New Testament.

'In the Universal Church there is the sacrifice of Jesus Christ, whose body and blood are truly contained in the sacrament of the altar under the forms of bread and wine.'

LATERAN IV (12TH ECUMENICAL COUNCIL), CANON 1, 1215

A pyx – a receptacle created to hold the consecrated host – was an extremely early Christian art form because of its intimate involvement in one of the two original sacraments, the Eucharist. Early belief, as well as later Catholic and Eastern Orthodox traditions, stressed that the blessing of the priest transubstantiated the bread – literally turning it into the body of Christ – as the wine was literally turned into his blood. This belief made the consecrated host of utmost religious importance, and a special vessel was needed to hold the communion wafers either on the altar or hanging above it. A hanging pyx often took the form of a dove – a custom that originated in the East in late antiquity – representing the Holy Spirit of the Trinity, but it was also often constructed as a round box, such as this silver gilt example from the late Middle Ages. In modern Catholicism, the pyx is most often associated with the Viaticum, which is the offering of the Eucharist to the dying. As part of the last rites, the host has to be transported to the mortally ill and is stored in a pyx, which now usually takes the form of a small, flat, circular container about the size of a pocket watch. Historically, both the pyx and its consecrated contents are the subject of many miracles known as Eucharistic miracles. Caesarius of Heisterbach and many others have written of miracles such as the Bleeding Host, in which the host miraculously starts to bleed, proof that it is the literal flesh of Christ. In another account, a pyx and its contents are miraculously recognized by an ox that will not continue ploughing when it sees it in front of him.

# David

*c.* 1440 CE  **Bargello Palace, Florence, Italy**

**COMMISSIONED BY**  The Medici family    **MATERIALS**  Bronze
**ARTIST**  Donato di Niccolò di Betto Bardi    **HEIGHT**  158 cm/62 ¼ in.

Donatello's *David* is a seminal piece of Western art even without its
religious significance. The first free-standing bronze and the first
male nude since antiquity, the work is also the bearer of religious
and political meanings. Donatello was apprenticed to bronze
expert Lorenzo Ghiberti in 1404. By the time he produced his
bronze statue of *David* he was at the pinnacle of his technical skill.
The statue demonstrates a growing fascination with the classical
inheritance, one of the characteristics of the Renaissance that
was highlighted in Italy, with its proximity to Roman examples.
Despite the classical aesthetic, the subject of the work is the Old
Testament story of David and Goliath from 1 Samuel 17. Donatello
chose to portray the moment just after victory; he shows David's
foot resting delicately on Goliath's head and Goliath's sword in
his hand. This is combined with an inscription that reminds the
viewer that 'Kingdoms fall through luxury, cities rise through
virtues; behold the neck of pride severed by humility.' Donatello's
Medici patrons, who were being criticized for their increasingly
authoritarian rule, used this work to co-opt the biblical story of
religious authority winning over a physically stronger opponent.
1 Samuel describes David as a healthy and handsome boy, a
feature that Donatello emphasizes in an effeminate depiction of
late boyhood in Italy, at a time when men were not considered to
reach full manhood or marriageable age until their mid twenties.
After the fall of the Medici family, the work remained in Florence
and was moved to various locations, including the Pitti Palace and
the Uffizi, before being housed at the Bargello Palace.

### David and Goliath

David and Goliath's theme of
the earthly power of spiritual
authority is a popular one. The
victory of the Israelites over
the Philistines because of a
young boy was inspirational to
contemplate and illustrated the
triumph of good over evil. It was
popular with ruling elites who
identified themselves with David.

'This figure is so natural in
its vivacity and its softness,
that it is almost impossible
for craftsmen to believe
that it was not moulded
on the living form.'

GIORGIO VASARI,
*LIVES OF THE ARTISTS*

# Rosary Bead

1500 CE **Metropolitan Museum of Art, New York, USA**

**ORIGIN** Brabant, Netherlands **ARTIST** Not known
**MATERIAL** Boxwood **DIAMETER** 5.2 cm/2 in.

## Boxwood Triptych

Another example of an intricately carved boxwood piece from Brabant, from the same period, is this miniature triptych intended for devotional practices.

'Beware of thinking of the Rosary as something of little importance. ... Far from being insignificant, the Rosary is a priceless treasure which is inspired by God.'

ST LOUIS DE MONTFORT, *THE SECRET OF THE ROSARY* (1716)

The origins of rosary beads can be traced back to prayer ropes used by desert monks in the 3rd century. However, it was not until the later Middle Ages and early modern period that rosary beads and the Rosary prayer associated with them became integral to Roman Catholicism. The word 'rosary' comes from the Latin *rosarium* meaning 'crown of roses'. Pope Pius V made 7 October a feast day to celebrate the Rosary in the mid 16th century. He established an official set (known as a decade) of fifteen mysteries – the events in the lives of Christ and the Virgin Mary that are contemplated between prayers. In 2002, the number of mysteries was raised to twenty by Pope John Paul II. Rosary beads are used to help keep track of the mysteries, but also the individual prayers that make up the Rosary, which include Hail Marys, the Lord's Prayer and the Glory Be to the Father. This prayer bead from the early 16th century is proof of the growing popularity of the Rosary, as well as general devotion to Christ through Mary. Carved in the Duchy of Brabant in the southern Netherlands while it was under the rule of the Hapsburgs, this bead displays the intricate, small carvings in fine-grained boxwood for which the region was famous. When closed, the bead displays the crown of thorns. When the inner doors are closed it, there is a scene depicting Adam and Eve. The open doors form a triptych, seen here, that displays scenes from the Nativity, an appropriate subject for a rosary bead. The bottom scene is the Crucifixion, another of the mysteries that are contemplated when saying the Rosary. When not in use rosary beads could be worn around the neck or waist.

## Our Lady of Guadalupe

1531 CE **Basilica of Our Lady of Guadalupe, Mexico City, Mexico**

**ORIGIN** Mexico City   **ARTIST** Not known
**MATERIALS** Tempera on linen hemp   **HEIGHT** 1.75 m/5 ¾ ft

### Modern Basilica

A new Basilica of Our Lady of Guadalupe was completed in 1976 to house the original *tilma* of Juan Diego, who was canonized in 2002. The new basilica has a circular floor plan 100 metres (350 ft) in diameter to enable views of the *tilma* from all parts of the building. The basilica is the most visited Marian shrine in the world, attracting millions of visitors especially around the feast day on 12 December.

'This New World has been won and conquered by the hand of the Virgin Mary.'

FATHER MIGUEL SÁNCHEZ (1648)

On 9 December 1531, only about a decade after Hernán Cortés conquered Mexico, indigenous Indian Juan Diego saw a vision of a girl who revealed herself to be the Virgin Mary at the Hill of Tepeyac. The Spanish archbishop of Mexico City, Juan de Zumárraga, demanded proof that the woman Juan Diego had seen was the Virgin; she responded by healing Juan Diego's uncle and causing a miraculous growth of Castilian roses. The Virgin put these roses in Juan's *tilma* (cloak) and when he opened it in front of the archbishop, the image of Our Lady of Guadalupe was revealed. Scholars disagree about whether the Spanish name Guadalupe was the original or a translation of an indigenous Nahuatl name, but either way the acheiropoieta (icons not made by a human hand) soon became the famous heart of the basilica in Mexico City that shares her name. While later gilding and overpainting have been scientifically proven, none of the investigations undertaken have been able to explain the unusually bright colours nor how such a delicate fabric survives intact almost half a millennium later. Although an early symbol of successful Spanish conquest and conversion, in the 19th and 20th centuries Guadalupe became a Mexican national symbol associated with Father Miguel Hidalgo in 1810 and Emiliano Zapata during the Mexican Revolution of 1910. Today her basilica receives the most pilgrims of any Catholic site, with a record 6.1 million pilgrims on the anniversary of the apparition in 2009. Her popularity has since transcended national borders, with churches dedicated to her ranging from Wisconsin in the United States to Canelones in Uruguay.

# Hand of St Teresa of Avila

1582 CE **Convento de Santa Teresa, Avila, Spain**

**ORIGIN** Avila, Spain   **ARTIST** Not known
**MATERIALS** Mixed metals, glass, precious stones

St Teresa of Avila was born into a *marrano* (Jewish convert) family and, as if proving she was not a lapsed convert, she took each aspect of her Christianity to the greatest degree possible. Educated by Augustinian nuns, she felt that the convents were too lax and, with permission, began establishing reformed convents that emphasized absolute poverty. In 1576 she was forced to retire to her foundation in Toledo and came under investigation by the Inquisition, but her letters to Philip II resulted in her freedom and she spent her final years founding new convents. However, it is for her mystical experiences of God through devotion, and her many autobiographical writings describing and explaining them, that she achieved her high religious status. From the time she first entered the convent she experienced visions and mystical experiences, some of which involved Christ appearing invisibly but physically to her. She described the path of devotion as four stages of the soul: mental prayer, prayer of quiet, devotion of union and devotion of ecstasy. These stages involve slowly giving over to God the capacities of one's mind: will, reason, memory and imagination. After reaching the final stage the devotee faints and wakes with tears known as the 'blessing of tears', proof of a mystical experience. Teresa was canonized in 1622 and in 1970 Pope Paul VI made St Teresa and St Catherine of Siena the first female Doctors of the Church. Her relics, such as this one that is housed in a convent built over her birthplace, are scattered all over the world and are revered for their seeming lack of decay, regarded as a sign of sanctity.

## Bernini's The Ecstasy of St Teresa

St Teresa's description of her vision inspired one of the most famous works by Gian Lorenzo Bernini, *The Ecstasy of St Teresa*. It powerfully depicts her ecstatic union with God when an angel pierces her heart and she feels the sweetness of pain.

'The pain was so great, that it made me moan; and yet so surpassing was the sweetness of this excessive pain, that I could not wish to be rid of it.'

ST TERESA OF AVILA

# Botafumeiro

1851 CE  **Cathedral of Santiago de Compostela, Galicia, Spain**

**ARTIST** José Losada    **MATERIALS** Silver-plated brass and bronze
**WEIGHT** 80 kg/176 lb    **HEIGHT** 1.6 m/5¼ ft

## Catherine of Aragon

The rope holding the Botafumeiro must be replaced every few decades or accidents occur. The most famous occasion was when it crashed through a window while being swung in the presence of Catherine of Aragon, who stopped on her way to marry Arthur Tudor, Prince of Wales.

'Incense serves to show the effect of grace, wherewith Christ was filled as with a good odour according to Genesis 27:27.'

ST THOMAS AQUINAS,
*SUMMA THEOLOGICA* (1265–74)

Scent has played an important role in Christian liturgy from its earliest days. This role is performed by incense, which is burned in containers known as censers. These are swung to release their aroma during Mass, marriages, the consecration of altars, ceremonies honouring a saint's tomb or over the deceased at funerals. This practice reaches back to at least the early 4th century when church records list gifts of censers and incense. Although the Reformation reduced the use of incense in Christianity, it had been so ubiquitous in the Middle Ages that when figures were shown in an image with a censer it demonstrated their sanctity. Incense was also believed to have a cleansing effect in times of plague and epidemics. The Botafumeiro, which means 'smoke expeller' in Galician, is one of the world's largest examples of a thurible, or metal censer, hung from chains. The tradition of using a censer at the Cathedral of Santiago de Compostela in Galicia goes back to the 12th century. A 15th-century thurible donated to the cathedral by France's King Louis XI was stolen by Napoleon's forces in 1809 and a new one was not created for more than forty years, when gold and silversmith José Losada created this one. However, the pulley system that operates the censer, and which is still in use, dates to 1604. The Botafumeiro is kept in the library of the cathedral, but is brought out for traditional feast days and when tourist or religious groups to the pilgrimage site pay a fee. The fee is used to pay for the 40 kg (88 lb) of incense and charcoal that are used each time, as well as the work of the *tiraboleiros* – the eight men in red robes who carry and swing the Botafumeiro.

# Index

# Picture Credits

# About the author

Heather Thornton McRae teaches history at the University of Missouri. She specializes in medieval Iberia, but has published papers on a diverse range of subjects – from religion in the Viking Age to Albertus Magnus's theories on physiognomy.